Gone - Catastrophe In Paradise

Gone

Catastrophe In Paradise

O.J. Modjeska

About the Author

OJ Modjeska is a historian, criminologist, and author. She graduated from the University of Sydney with a PhD in Modern American History in 2004, and received her Graduate Diploma in Criminology from Sydney Law School in 2015. In 2015 she was awarded the JH McClemens Memorial Prize by Sydney Law School for her scholarship in criminology. Before pursuing a writing career she worked for many years as a legal writer and editor. OJ writes books of narrative non-fiction true crime and disaster analysis. Her debut, "Gone: Catastrophe in Paradise", about the Tenerife air disaster, is an ebook bestseller. "A City Owned" and "Killing Cousins" make up the two-part true crime series "Murder by Increments", now available at all good ebook retailers. If you enjoy this book and would like to receive news of new releases, consider subscribing to OJ's mailing list at the link below.

http://ojmodjeska.blogspot.com.au

www.estoire.co

Publication Details

First published in 2017 by Estoire

Text © OJ Modjeska (Obelia Modjeska), 2017

Ecclesiastes 9:11-12

"I have seen something else under the sun:
The race is not to the swift or the battle to the strong,
nor does food come to the wise or wealth to the brilliant or favor to the learned;
but time and chance happen to them all.
Moreover, no man knows when his hour will come:
As fish are caught in a cruel net,
or birds are taken in a snare,
so men are trapped by evil times that fall unexpectedly upon them."
Ecclesiastes 9:11-12

Foreword

Forty years ago, on the afternoon of 27 March 1977, a mass of American and European tourists descended on a tropical paradise for the holiday of a lifetime. Within hours, hundreds were dead.

The events described in this book are well known to people inside the aviation community. The Tenerife airport disaster was, and remains, the deadliest airplane accident in history. The twin towers disaster of 2001 incurred a greater loss of life, but because that event was the result of deliberate sabotage, it has never been classed as an "accident". The death toll of the Tenerife tragedy, 583 people, thus still stands as the worst on record in terms of aviation mishaps.

I have always been fascinated by this disaster. The story within in it is not only devastatingly tragic, but really rather bizarre. The calamity was preceded by an almost inconceivable chain of ironies and the unlikeliest of coincidences. It has always surprised me, however, that most people I speak to casually know little or nothing about Tenerife. And the public accounts that are available don't really get across what it so fascinating about it.

I wrote this book with a vision to bring the real story of Tenerife to a wider audience: to folk who aren't particularly informed about aviation history, those who aren't avid devotees of *Air Crash Investigations*, *Mayday*, *Seconds from Disaster* and the various technical reports that are available—but are also rather dull to read.

Several short written accounts of this disaster exist, but they are generally prosaic and dry, scientific analyses of an event that has an incredible human dimension which is often overlooked.

The field of disaster analysis remains unevolved in the literary sense. Here I have attempted to create an account that takes the reader right inside the events of that afternoon, to reveal how they might have been experienced by the key players involved: the cockpit crews, the passengers and the tower controllers. I also wanted to relate the sad but also extremely inspiring story of the aftermath of this disaster, those events that transpired in the days immediately following the crash, on the mysterious little island of Tenerife. That story has been neglected in previous accounts, and without knowing it, the true nature of the entire event is obscured from view.

It will be up to the reader whether I have done my subject justice. Hopefully the result of my efforts is not just informative, but a journey to travel ...

Chapter 1

"We're going!" says the captain, spooling up his engines.

In the rear of the Boeing 747, the passengers are relieved to be finally getting off the ground, having spent the better part of three hours stranded during an unscheduled stop. This airline, like all of them, promises efficiency and on-time travel. The promotional literature tucked in the back of the seats brags confidently about their safety record and reputation for getting their passengers where they need to go, when they need to get there.

Nobody stops to ponder the occasionally contradictory nature of these aims.

Just as fate would have it, our captain is now enslaved in the grip of irreconcilable goals, impossible expectations. Yet this fact remain beneath his awareness.

He has just spent the last several hours feeling irritable beyond words, in a place he never intended to go, and will happily never see again—and now, all he can think about is the fact he is about to get up into the skies. He's *made* it. They're outta there.

But in his haste, he has overlooked one crucial piece of information: he has never actually been given clearance to take off.

Seconds later, the pilot of another 747, similarly loaded with passengers and still taxiing on the active runway, sights the grim specter of expanding orbs of light through the fog. In a grotesque flash of insight, all becomes clear.

"There he is!" he cries, pushing the thrust levers to full power, desperately trying to steer his massive charge out of the path of carnage. "Look at him! That son of a bitch is coming!"

* * *

We humans tend to think about fate or destiny in positive terms. When something wonderful and unexpected happens—a lottery win, being offered a dream job, meeting your soulmate randomly on a street corner—we say that the stars aligned, we finally got our lucky break, and by some miracle the perfect ingredients of happenstance came together to grant our most fervently held dreams.

But what about those occasions that represent the unhappy results of the rarest chain of coincidence? Those times when the stars did indeed align—but instead, for the perfect storm?

Nobody likes to think about those situations. After all, they throw a grim challenge to our sense of hope, to our belief in the basically benevolent design of the universe. Instead, they seem to point darkly to the existence of malicious deities, to an indifferent—even hostile—world.

The story I am about to tell you concerns just this kind of incident.

Chapter 2

The Stage is Set

We are not in the present, but some four decades in the past. The society and its inhabitants are only superficially unfamiliar. Do not be deceived by nostalgia or regret for innocence lost. Probe a little deeper and you will learn much about where we have come from, and just how we got to where we are now.

Americans are enjoying for the first time the benefits of affordable international air travel and, along with it, mass tourism. Jumping on a flight and heading off for an overseas jaunt is becoming a middle-class thing to do.

Along with the optimism and sense of adventure, there is trepidation. Terrorism has been rearing its head in recent years, making uncomfortable inroads into everyday life. It is five years since the Munich Massacre of 1972: star Olympic athletes captured and killed by Palestinian nationalists, hundreds of innocents taken captive. In its wake, a wave of fear and impotence ripples through the West. In two years there will be a critical tipping point in the evolution of Islamic radicalism, very visibly brought home to Americans in the form of the Iranian hostage crisis. A president widely regarded as ineffectual is unable to return his fellow Americans to safety. A corroding wound to national self-esteem ensues.

Our unwary passengers are caught in the crosshairs of this unfolding historical drama.

They are destined for the Canaries, a regional hub for tourism of the joyful and sun-drenched kind. The Canary Islands, an Atlantic archipelago just off the Moroccan coastline, is a holiday destination much favoured by European and American vacationers since the tourist boom of the 1960s.

Historically it has been sometimes referred to as the Land of Eternal Spring or the Fortunate Isles, the latter deriving from the title of an epic poem from the sixteenth century by Antonio Viviana, a native of La Laguna on Tenerife. The many international visitors are attracted by the warm, sunny climate and the beaches, and continue to imagine that the name of the islands has something to do with the delightful yellow tropical bird, the canary.

This is a common misconception. In fact the name for the bird comes from the name of the islands, which means "Islands of the Dogs". Pliny the Younger reported that the Berber king Juba II sent an expedition to the islands, and named them for the particularly ferocious native breed of canines that greeted his contingent on their arrival.

This story evokes a certain truth about the Canaries, relating to all that is hidden by its popular image as a tropical paradise and playpen for sun-worshippers. Scratch the surface and this place has a strange and mysterious side to it, not to mention a complex and bloody history that tourists for the most part very much prefer to ignore.

Despite the year-round sunshine, parts of the islands can become suddenly and unpredictably fogbound. The balmy climate is a result of latitude and the tradewinds, which concentrate humidity over parts of the archipelago into vast, low-flying banks of cloud that range between 600 and 1800 meters in height. The rocky and mountainous nature of the islands, forged over million years of volcanic formation, contribute too to the unpredictable patterns of wind, rain and low cloud. Politically, the islands have been subject to bitter territorial disputes between Berbers and the Spanish who have controlled them since the Castilian conquests. In what is to come, all these factors will come together in an unforeseeable, and most unfortunate, interplay of events.

The passengers are shortly to arrive at Las Palmas on Gran Canaria, the springboard for international flights to and from the Canaries, and the departure point for major cruise liners traveling to destinations in the Mediterranean, North Africa and South America.

But on the fateful day, shortly before they are due to touch down, a bomb explodes at a florist's shop on the main concourse of the international terminal at Las Palmas airport.

The scene is total chaos. There is significant damage to the inside of the terminal, now littered with shattered glass, shards of broken plaster and terrified humans that dart in all directions until some sense of order can be restored. Eight people are seriously injured.

A telephone call arrives at a service desk hinting at the presence of a second bomb located somewhere inside the terminal.

The mystery caller is a member of the Canary Islands separatists, formally the Canary Islands Independence Movement (CIIM).

CIIM, based in Algeria, are engaged in various violent actions against the Spanish. This attack on the terminal is one of many such gestures of fury and vindictiveness deemed richly deserved. In the sunset days of empire, all over the world the oppressed and dispossessed are launching campaigns against their collapsing European masters, seeking independence for places they call home. CIIM bring ideologies of Islamic radicalism in service of their goal of returning the Canaries to the original Berber inhabitants. They frequently target their attacks against the symbols of modernity and internationalization, air travel and tourism.

As much as they desire to inflict disruption and carnage, they can have no idea of the scale of disaster they are about to unleash.

With the threat of another bomb, as yet undetected, somewhere in the airport the Spanish authorities immediately evacuate the terminal and implement a directive to divert all incoming aircraft to Los Rodeos on the neighboring island of Tenerife.

Miguel Torrens is on duty at Las Palmas approach. He later explained that in his view the situation at Las Palmas was so alarming and chaotic that the authorities simply made a unilateral decision to divert all the aircraft to Los Rodeos, despite the fact that this solution was not without its own problems.

There was no leeway in the directive; an exception was made for two Iberia flights because they could disembark their passengers via a hangar at Las Palmas, rather than through the terminal. *Why could this not be done with other flights?* Torrens asked, his hands raised in a gesture of helplessness and futility. He didn't know.

Los Rodeos is a small regional airport. Its airstrips and facilities are designed to accommodate smaller planes of the type that complete short haul flights in and around the Canaries. It has only one runway—strictly two, runway 12 and runway 30. They form one continuous stretch of tarmac, laid out end to end. There is one major parallel taxiway. The main taxiway and runway are joined by four smaller taxiways. Visualize an oblong crossed over the middle with little white lines.

Now, all of a sudden, a stream of large wide body jets from international carriers are arriving, rerouted from Las Palmas, and waiting to land at the tiny airport.

Fernando Azcunaga and just one other controller are on duty in the tower at Los Rodeos, approaching the end of their shift after a busy day.

From time to time they have been called on to accept diverted traffic, and it is all well and good that they accommodate one or two Boeing 747s on their tiny parking apron. But this is an entirely different story; there are several large jets circling above, waiting to land, with more to arrive. It is a situation they are unused to. Already the men are starting to sweat.

Azcunaga, a Spanish national from the Basque region, is an experienced professional, having worked as a controller since 1964—well over a decade. He's used to dealing with substandard equipment and long shifts due to under-staffing, but he loves his job. Some twenty years after the disaster he summed up the working conditions for controllers at Los Rodeos at the time with one well-chosen, powerfully descriptive word: "atrocious".

The communications equipment broke down all the time, he reminisced with his disarming chuckle. *The tower wasn't even soundproof. We could hear cars on the road outside!*

The airport at Los Rodeos also presents a number of idiosyncrasies that make Azcunaga's job uniquely challenging.

There is, in fact, a little folk tale about the airport's origins, the truth or otherwise of which has never really been established. For the people of Tenerife, the story is a mildly amusing joke, a comment on the absurdity of life. Allegedly the original planners marked an "X" on a map to mark the place which, due to the awkwardness of the terrain and the prevalence of fog and inclement weather, they believed an airport should never, ever be built.

Later, another planning group took over the project, and mistook this X for the opposite. One of the world's most inhospitable airports was born.

Los Rodeos is located 2073 feet above sea level, and clouds that are normally 200 feet above sea level are here on the ground. The thick clouds roll down the nearby mountains onto the runways, resulting in rapidly changing visibility conditions. The local high terrain also causes the so-called venturi effect. Increased wind speed and decreased pressure increases the cloud density.

There is, at this time, no ground radar at the airport, so Azcunaga and his colleagues are sometimes in the position of directing traffic on the ground that they cannot even see. He relies on the cockpit crews to accurately report their position.

At around 1:30 pm, Azcunaga receives a request for landing clearance from a KLM jet. The KLM is a Boeing 747, registration PH-BUF, carrying the stately formal moniker of the *Rhine*. It has departed Schipol Airport in Amsterdam at nine in the morning carrying 234 passengers, mostly young Dutch nationals escaping the cold northern winter for holidays in the Canaries. There are two Australians, four Germans and four Americans. Amongst the passengers are 48 children—and three babies.

By this time several international flights have already landed at Los Rodeos. With limited space to accommodate them, Azcunaga directs them to the parking apron situated between the main taxiway and the holding point for runway 12. Very quickly the parking apron is full, and the planes start spilling out onto the main taxiway parallel to the active runway.

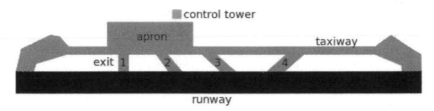

After landing, the KLM taxis across the last intersecting taxiway to clear the runway and parks behind a Norwegian Boeing 737 ahead of it in the queue. Once Las Palmas reopens, KLM will have to wait for several planes ahead of it to take off, since the parked planes block the path to the only active runway.

Azcunaga is up against it. From one point of view this is just an ordinary day at work—stress, lots of problems to solve, potential chaos that must be forced into a shape of order and predictability. This is the life of any controller. From another perspective, it isn't a normal day at all. The circumstances are unprecedented in his experience, and layered with complexity and the potential for strife.

Who knows how long it will be before Las Palmas reopens? How many more planes will arrive?

It is not a good situation for anyone—not for him, nor any of the crews operating the jets down on the ground. Vaguely, he worries about the possibility of a terrorist attack on Los Rodeos itself. With all the traffic now crowding the small airport, and passengers now disembarking the planes and flooding the small terminal, such an eventuality would be disastrous.

Even with all the problems confronting him, what is in fact about to transpire is the furthest thing from his mind.

* * *

Some twenty minutes after the KLM lands, a Pan American 747 makes its way across from Las Palmas in line with its instructions from Las Palmas approach, and radios to the ground for its landing clearance.

This vessel is carrying 380 passengers, most of whom are retirees bound for a cruise aboard the *Golden Odyssey*, departing from Las Palmas and making stops at ports in North Africa and Greece. The vast majority have boarded at Los Angeles, where the flight originated. An additional fourteen step on at New York's John F. Kennedy International Airport.

The journey started with an air of buzz and excitement, given a boost by the presence of a celebrity on board, the almost unfeasibly buxom Hollywood pin-up girl, Eve Meyer. But the ambience in the cabin sharply deteriorates with this unexpected disruption to their plans.

These are people who have worked tirelessly all their lives to enjoy the peace and freedom of their autumn years, and they are very much looking forward to their holiday. Now, they don't know when or if this much anticipated fling upon the Mediterranean's sapphire seas will be happening. Vaguely, some worry about the impact of an indefinite delay on their ability to make their connection. The buoyant mood has given way to lethargy and irritation.

In the captain's seat of the Pan American *Clipper* is Victor Grubbs of Centerport, New York, fifty-seven but fighting fit. On 23 March, a few days earlier, he passes his medical exam with no apparent issues. He holds the standard ATP license and licenses to pilot the Boeing 747 and its narrow-body forerunner the 707. He's got more than twenty thousand flying hours under his belt, and half a thousand on the Boeing 747 specifically. Since this particular kind of airplane has only been in service for six years, that's quite a lot.

Grubbs is a no-nonsense type. Diligent, level-headed, somewhat reserved. Characters thus constituted arguably make the best kinds of pilots. Their ambitions are delineated purely by mastery of the technology and a sense of custodianship for their crew and passengers. No ego, no fanfare. Just get the job done, then go home and rest.

Despite a touch of shyness, he is possessed of a quiet magnetism. *He filled a room when he walked into it*, a flight attendant later recalled. *It was obvious to everyone that he was someone special, quiet, unflappable, with a wry sense of the absurd.*

Grubbs shies away from the limelight. In years to come, he will give very few interviews.

Some will speculate he is simply so badly affected by the tragedy, he can't even bring himself to speak of it.

He adores his mighty charge, the *Clipper*, thus christened by First Lady Pat Nixon. What a beauty she is; a magnificent example of design. The Boeing 747 is a mammoth of the skies, a metal hulk that flies like the lightest of birds. But the *Clipper* is one very special 747. She is the first one rolled-out to the travelling public. She made the maiden voyage of the Boeing 747 from New York to London's Heathrow just seven years earlier, on 15 January 1970. A small dent remains on the nose of the plane, where a champagne bottle was flung against it in celebration.

Grubbs and his employer Pan American World Airways enjoy a long relationship of reciprocal loyalty and trust. Pan American is the flagship national carrier of the Unites States, and has been in operation since 1927. Despite heavy financial losses and organizational realignments in the wake of the oil crisis of the early seventies, this is an exciting time for the airline during which it expands and innovates to meet the demands of a market burgeoning under the new influences of mass tourism and global enterprise. The new business model is built around the concept of affordable international travel for the average American. The Pan American brand makes every American proud.

Part of what has made Pan American a success story is its unique organizational culture. Compared to many airlines, it is not particularly hierarchical, at least as far as standard operating crew are concerned—pilots, engineers, ground crew and flight attendants. At a time when military organizational principles still hold sway in the airline industry, and the majority of commercial pilots are recruited from the excess pool of former air force personnel no longer needed at the end of a long and brutal war, Pan American's style is refreshingly democratic. The crews are known for their experience and rigorous training across multiple roles within the company. At Pan American nobody is better than any particular job or task. All is considered good training. A typical captain might begin his career years earlier as a radio operator or even mechanic, gaining his licenses steadily over time and eventually rising to the rank of navigator, second officer and first officer. Prior to the Second World War, a captain making engine repairs at a remote location was an unremarkable event.

The organizational discipline of Crew Resource Management (CRM), a set of safety techniques to improve communication and decision-making in cockpits, is not yet in currency in the airline industry, but Pan American already employs an embryonic form of CRM due to its organizational culture. Generally, their cockpit culture is one in which the various members of a team feel safe to offer feedback on decisions—or even question a decision made by the most senior ranking individual in a cockpit: the captain. In just the last five years or so, the airline management have made a number of recommendations in the wake of a number of pilot error incidents in the Pacific. The foremost of these is so-called crew concept training. The idea is that cockpit activities are being reconceived as team responsibilities. Pan American's manuals have been revised to incorporate crew concepts and to provide a more comprehensive explanation of accountabilities for team activities and communications. This is in fact a fundamental and very positive change of direction.

The vastly differing cockpit cultures at Pan American and KLM are plain to hear in the CVR recording of the horrific drama to come. One team can be heard casually conversing throughout the build-up to the incident, comparing notes on incoming information and the decisions they need to take. In the KLM cockpit there is comparative silence. Conversation is intermittent, formal and stilted.

* * *

Azcunaga clears the *Clipper* to land at Los Rodeos, which it does at around 2:00 pm. After cooling its jets and making its way down runway 12, it crosses a Charlie taxiway over to the parallel major taxiway and joins the other planes on the crowded parking apron. The Pan American has arrived immediately after the KLM *Rhine*, and parks immediately behind it. This means that, should Las Palmas reopen soon, *Clipper* will have to wait for KLM to depart before it can move. KLM is blocking its path to the active runway.

For the Pan American crew, the news that they would not be able to land at Las Palmas was rather unwelcome. This was first signified by their request to circle in the sky above Las Palmas until it reopened, a request that was flatly denied.

They have now been on duty for nearly eight hours since boarding at New York, and the unscheduled stop at Las Palmas will add considerable length to their shift. They are, as yet, not approaching their duty time limit—this is the stipulated maximum of hours they can be working before they will be in breach of airline industry codes implemented in the interests of safety.

At this point, the team in the cockpit—Grubbs, First Officer Robert Bragg and Flight Engineer George Warns—are more concerned about the passengers. Most of them are elderly people, and unlike the cockpit crew, the majority boarded the flight at its originating city Los Angeles. They've already been travelling for 13 hours, and they are getting tired.

Karen Anderson is sitting halfway up the back of the cabin, near the wing.

How were we feeling? Well, mostly just frustrated. It had been a really long trip. I was tired. I just wanted to get off this plane. I was sad and frustrated that we couldn't immediately disembark.

It wasn't as if the crew or the passengers had any sense that something terrible was about to take place. On the other hand, the situation that was materializing was one of annoyance, fatigue—and potentially confusion.

Some passengers are more uneasy about what is taking place than others. For many the feeling is purely one of irritation. For others there is a vague intuition that they have stumbled into a situation ripe with the potential for unhappy developments.

A person knowledgeable about aviation, or even just the average observant individual, could certainly be aware that the crowded condition of the airport was not conducive to safety. Warren Hopkins, also aboard the Pan Am, later spoke some rather chilling words.

People were not happy about this. It was not a good omen, you know. It was not a good omen having this take place.

Still, the Pan American crew are optimistic that they'll get off the ground again soon, and onto their final destination Las Palmas. Given this they take the decision to keep their passengers on board, at least until notice of any further developments. When they are given permission to move, they want to be in a position to do so quickly.

Looking out the windows, the passengers on the plane are greeted by a rather different sight to what they expect of a place renowned as paradise on earth. Tenerife is indeed an island of unusual beauty, replete with white sandy beaches, lazily swaying palms, blue skies and colorful tropical flora. But the view from the plane is of a barren and dry place, flat and uninspiring but for the vaguely ominous mountains looming in the distance. Nothing is happening here but the tiresome and repetitive arrival of one plane after another, similarly stranded with no place to go.

To distract and entertain the tired and grumpy passengers, Grubbs invites them to peer into the cockpit and learn more about operations from the flight crew. In the wake of 9-11 this practice is now against regulations, but in the seventies, it was a common exercise. The flight attendants also open some doors on the plane so people can look outside and take fresh air without leaving the cabin.

Meanwhile, the passengers on the KLM are allowed to off-board the plane and wander around in the terminal.

This group of passengers are also looking forward to a holiday. The flight has been chartered by the Holland International Travel Group (HINT) to carry Dutch nationals to vacations in the Canaries organised by the tour operator.

Amongst the travelers is Robina Van Lanschott, a tour guide with HINT. She is accompanied by friends Walter and Yvonne. The three step off the jumbo and mosey into the terminal with the hundreds of other Dutch passengers who now begin crowding the small concourse and coffee shop. This isn't so bad, they are thinking: at least they can stretch their legs!

Robina, oddly enough, lives on Tenerife in the small fishing town of Puerto de la Cruz with her boyfriend. Their relationship is new and in the full bloom of young love.

She wonders aloud what her next move should be given that their flight has been unexpectedly diverted to Tenerife and she doesn't know how long it will be until Las Palmas reopens. What would be the point, she says to Walter and Yvonne, of flying onto Las Palmas since she is in Tenerife already?

— I want to go home, Robina says. I want to go today! I just love and miss him so much …

Yvonne and Walter urge Robina to reboard the plane with them and go onto Las Palmas. It will be fun, they say. They can have a drink and a meal together at the other end.

Robina remains undecided about what to do until the last moment.

* * *

The decision to deplane the passengers has been taken because the KLM flight crew, led by Captain Jacob Veldhuyzen Van Zanten, want to refuel at Los Rodeos. The passengers are unaware of the reasoning behind the decision to refuel, but that reasoning is also indicative of the negative potential of the situation developing at the airport.

The flight crew on the KLM plane are, in fact, approaching their duty time limit. They are scheduled to return to Amsterdam after stopping at Las Palmas within those limits. They call KLM headquarters in Amsterdam and verify that they have until 6:30 pm to return. This isn't an impossible timeframe, but it is tight—and who knows how long they are going to be delayed at Los Rodeos.

They need fuel for the return trip and think they can save time by refueling during this unscheduled layover, rather than doing it at Las Palmas. In other words, they are in something of a rush.

Our captain, a dignified and charismatic man, never fond of a situation out of control, sits in the cockpit scratching his nose and pondering his situation with growing unease.

He is anxious about the approaching duty time restriction. If they don't get off the ground soon and get to Las Palmas, he will have to find accommodation for all the passengers on tiny Tenerife and they will all be delayed overnight. There will be substantial costs and headaches involved for the airline.

Van Zanten is particularly sensitive to any negative repercussions for KLM if they don't get into the air soon due to his senior position with this airline. He is top of the food chain with KLM, in charge of both the training program for pilots and safety. Reputational and financial risks that face his company feel like personal threats.

Until quite recently, he would have been authorized to extend his crew's duty time limit to meet an unanticipated delay such as this. But following on from some recent incidents where crew fatigue posed risks to safety, the Dutch civil aviation authority have legislated provisions requiring strict observance of these limits. Captains who exceed them are now, in fact, exposed to prosecution.

The situation, then, presents a number of ironies. The duty time limits are legislated in the interests of passenger safety. In this instance those regulations cause the KLM crew to feel harried and want to get off the ground as fast as possible—which itself is a possible safety risk.

In the passenger cabin, the KLM brochures given to the passengers prominently display a picture of Van Zanten himself: handsome, blue eyed, smiling brightly like something out of a toothpaste commercial. Accompanying his picture is the tagline: "KLM. From the people who made punctuality possible". Not only is Van Zanten the top pilot at the airline, he's their official media mascot as well.

The passengers are excited and glad to learn that their captain today is the famous Van Zanten.

He's the face of KLM. What could make them feel safer?

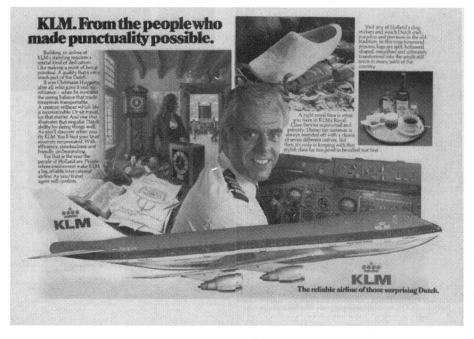

Well might we ask, what kind of man is this? For the answer to that question certainly carries significance in the matter at hand; the construction of this catastrophe.

It isn't an easy question to answer. History will prove him a divisive character. Some will condemn him a mass murderer, a pompous and reckless man convinced of his incapacity for error. Other, more moderate voices, will call him a victim of circumstance, a man of unimpeachable integrity who simply had a bad day.

Our frameworks of explanation tend to be riddled with suppositions born of prejudice and generalization. The mythology surrounding Tenerife is no exception. Fingers will be pointed. Blame will be cast. Voices thick with outrage and criticism will cry out and demand that someone, somewhere, must be accountable for such a horrendous tragedy.

Perhaps it was the arrogant, imperious Dutch, leaders of the world's oldest and safest airline, sure they could do no wrong. Or it was the lazy, incompetent Spaniards, distracted by their football game. Maybe we should blame the Americans; as usual, they were determined to come off as heroes—or victims, but they made their share of mistakes on that terrible, terrible afternoon.

The truth is never kind, nor easy. It will provide no succor to such childish demands for justice. Here, there is no ready scapegoat on which to heap scorn.

We make judgments about the past from the standpoint of the present. To characterize our captain as an arrogant man is to overlook that any such arrogance was entirely befitting his station, and a natural product of the cultural ethos that prevailed at his organisation.

Here are the facts: those who knew him said he was a remarkable human being. Characterized in broad measure by a methodical nature, sincerity, attention to detail. He was sober, introverted, yet open-hearted and friendly.

A perfect pilot, a good guy, and a great professional.

These words were spoken by Van Zanten's colleague, Ad de Bruin. He was as incredulous as anyone else at KLM that this mind-boggling disaster could have occurred.

Here are some more facts: at the time of this accident, Van Zanten has just returned from a six-month safety course for commercial pilots. He is the most experienced pilot at KLM, with over thirty years flying experience—but, in recent years, most of that experience has been within simulators, where he is training other pilots—not flying routes in the real world. In amongst all his experience and professionalism, here is his Achilles heel, a weak spot that bodes ill for his situational awareness within a complex real-life situation.

This is certainly an important factor, the influence of which will be brought to question in the autopsy of events to follow. But it is well to remember that is only as a result of what is about to take place that any questions will be asked about a captain's right to make unilateral decisions affecting his crew and passengers. Technology has made enormous strides, but the idea of the captain's role has not progressed too much further than days of traditional seafaring and military conquest. He is in charge.

And he can't be expected to overturn, in the interests of safety, a protocol and a way of doing things that is not yet, historically speaking, even open to question.

Some more facts: First Officer Klaas Meurs and Flight Engineer Willem Schreuder are unquestionably Van Zanten's subordinates. For Meurs, this is in fact his first journey as a co-pilot aboard a 747, although his experience traveling this same route is greater than Van Zanten's own, albeit on a different aircraft, the DC-8. As the chief pilot instructor at KLM, Van Zanten is indeed the individual who has approved Meurs' certification for his license to fly the Boeing 747.

Meurs would have been in awe of this individual, and perhaps reluctant to question his authority—although try he does.

* * *

In the Los Rodeos control tower, good news finally arrives at 4:00 pm, some twenty minutes after the *Clipper* lands. After all the inconvenience of diverting the planes, it happens that a thorough search of the terminal at Las Palmas has found no trace of a second bomb.

The caller from CIIM was bluffing.

Following this, the authorities at Las Palmas decide to reopen the terminal. In light of what has occurred, it might have made more sense to allow the planes to circle above Los Rodeos, a decision which would have prevented the impending catastrophe. But of course, nobody could have known that things were going to turn out so deceptively well.

Fernando Azcunaga is pleased that he can start moving all these enormous planes off his crowded parking apron and send them back to Las Palmas. He is already looking forward to a well-deserved rest and a more routine day at work tomorrow.

But the decision to reopen Las Palmas by no means signifies an end to his struggles. He now has to coordinate the very complicated logistics of getting the planes off the ground with limited room for them to roll and takeoff. Because several of the planes are parked on the parallel taxiway, it means that the remaining open portion of tarmac, the runway itself, must be used for both taxiing and takeoff.

This procedure is known as a "backtaxi" or backtrack, and while not an ideal method for performing a takeoff, it is a quite respectable alternative. It involves taxiing down the runway, and making a complete turn so the plane is positioned for a takeoff roll back in the opposite direction.

At very small airstrips, backtaxiing is done as a matter of course because of the absence of any separate taxiway. At any major international or regional controlled airport, pilots are unauthorized to backtaxi unless such is specifically requested by the controller. This is because backtracking on a runway that does have connected taxiways populated by moving aircraft can indeed give rise to situations of peril.

As things stand, Azcunaga and his colleague don't have a choice.

* * *

A short while later, the Pan Am and KLM crews are advised by the tower that Las Palmas has reopened and is accepting traffic again. They will soon be on their way.

This news should be major cause for celebration for Jacob Van Zanten. It brings an end to his worries about breaching duty time restrictions and having to put all his passengers up for the night on Tenerife. Certainly, he is relieved. But because he has now taken the decision to refuel his aircraft, he will still be detained a little longer. Ironically, the news that Las Palmas has reopened comes just five minutes after he has begun refueling.

The refueling will take a good half an hour to complete. Additionally, all his passengers who have temporarily disembarked need time to re-board the plane. All of this means that he and his crew and passengers will be stuck at Los Rodeos longer than they need to be; and the crews manning the planes parked behind him, prevented from accessing the runway by his massive jet, are also stuck.

They are not happy about this. To their minds, they are being further and unnecessarily delayed. The stressful conditions give rise to a bitter and ungenerous cast of mind. They peer out their windows at the huge white jet with its blue stripe, sitting there so resplendently, unconcerned for the struggles of the crews trapped behind. How smug he is, they think, wasting everybody's time like this.

Inside the terminal, Robina says goodbye to her friends Walter and Yvonne. A KLM representative has refused her request to have her ticket changed so she can terminate her journey at Los Rodeos. She is required to re-board by regulations, but Robina decides to flout the law and hightail it out of the terminal anyway.

What are they going to do, she says to Walter and Yvonne, laughing. Arrest her?

Walter tells Robina he will pick up her luggage at the other end. Not only does Robina never get her bags back, she will never see Walter and Yvonne again.

* * *

On the Pan American vessel, Grubbs, Warns and Bragg are trying to maintain their sense of humor. It isn't easy. They are weary and irritable, because they, too, are keen to get off the ground—but KLM and its refueling vehicle are blocking the path to the runway.

Several other planes, blessed by comparatively smaller size, are able to maneuver around the KLM and be on their way. The Pan Am crew watch them soar into the sky with impotent envy.

Their frustration mounting, they decide to take a more proactive approach. It's a long shot, being that their ship is just as large as the KLM, but what if they could somehow squeeze past him too?

Bragg and Warns, with Grubb's approval, decide to go down on the ground and check out the available distance they have to pass KLM. Grubbs tells them they are probably wasting their time; he is sure they don't have enough room. But it's worth a try.

The mission ends in disheartening confirmation of Grubb's suspicions. They are short just 3.7 meters. This, on top of Van Zanten's decision to refuel his plane, is another fateful and unlucky link in the chain. If Pan Am could have departed before KLM, all would have been prevented.

In the terminal, more delays for KLM. A call has been issued for all passengers to return, but some are missing. A couple notify a flight attendant that they have lost their two children, presumed to have wandered out of the terminal to explore. The attendant sends runway coordinator Roberto Alvarez out to look for the two kids. Much to his later regret, Alvarez locates them, and sends them aboard the plane with their parents.

I'll never forget that. If I hadn't found them, they'd be alive today.

With the missing passengers rounded up—with the exception of Robina, who fortunately for some reason was not missed—KLM begin making their preparations for departure. The refueling vehicle disappears to its hangar, the passenger staircase is secreted away on its buggy and the doors slam shut behind the last unfortunate stragglers to return.

The Pan Am flight crew hear KLM call the tower for its start and taxi clearance and know their refueling is complete and it is time for them to get going. As First Officer Bragg later explained, Pan Am were following close behind the KLM ship.

As soon as he requested his start and taxi clearance, we followed by our request for our taxi clearance, and we were given our taxi clearance like five minutes after.

Grubbs' announcement to his passengers that Las Palmas is finally reopen for traffic is greeted with ringing applause in the cabin. Now they can look forward to joining their cruise ship and getting a solid night's rest after the better part of 24 hours without proper sleep.

The enthusiasm in the cockpit, on the other hand, is short-lived. The next phase of their preparations for departure are to be sadly littered with complication.

Grubbs, Bragg and Warns are aware that the planes that have departed ahead of them have all been given taxi instructions in an alternating pattern. One plane is to backtrack down the runway, and make a 180-degree turn to get into position for a takeoff roll in the opposite direction. The plane immediately following it is to taxi down the runway and exit off one of the Charlie taxiways, and take that taxiway to meet up with the clear portion of the parallel major taxi way that leads to the holding point for runway 30.

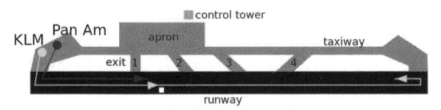

This decision has clearly been taken by the controllers for a couple of good reasons. Keep in mind that the major taxiway and the runway form a loop structure; but a large part of the major taxiway is populated with standing diverted aircraft. Taxiway C3 is the first one that will take an aircraft to the clear part of the main taxiway. A turnoff at an earlier taxiway would lead the plane concerned into the obstruction of parked planes. Azcunaga decides to instruct any plane following behind a backtracking plane to take C3.

In sum, this alternating pattern whereby one plane does a backtaxi and a 180-degree turn, and the next follows behind but departs the main runway via taxiway three to rejoin the runway via the main taxiway, is the only way to ensure the aircraft are able to depart in quick succession. Azcunaga could have each plane hold short of the runway and wait for the plane ahead of it to taxi, turn and take off; but it isn't his preference, as it will take much longer.

Sadly, his plan contains a hitch, as the Pan American crew are about to discover.

* * *

Captain Van Zanten, overjoyed to be moving at last, begins warming his engines for taxi. So far he has not been particularly impressed with the controllers or any of the staff at Los Rodeos. The whole experience, as far as he is concerned, has been unpleasantly chaotic and third rate. He isn't thinking too hard about the fact that these people are doing the best they can in difficult circumstances.

He finds Azcunaga's English difficult to understand. This compounds his irritation at the total experience of being delayed at Los Rodeos.

To say that it is an issue of racism or prejudice is probably unfair. This is simply a man who is used to having matters in hand, to operating in a controlled and regulated environment, the kind that KLM prides itself on providing for its staff and passengers. Van Zanten is the proverbial fish out of water. A man of high standards and expectations, stranded in an alien regional backwater, trying to figure out what the hell is going on.

To make matters worse, the tower now expresses confusion about the taxiing instructions. They seem to be caught in some dilemma about whether to direct KLM to perform a backtrack, or to place it on the route back to the runway via a Charlie taxiway turn off onto the main parallel taxiway.

This is an excerpt from the CVR transcript, clearly showing the uncertainty. KLM radios to the tower for confirmation of the directive.

—Approach KLM 4805 on the ground in Tenerife.

—KLM, ah, 4805, roger.

—We require backtrack on 12 for takeoff Runway 30.

—Okay, 4805 ... taxi ... to the holding position for Runway 30. Taxi into the runway and, ah, leave runway (third) to your left.

—Roger, sir, (entering) the runway at this time and the first (taxiway) we, we go off the runway again for the beginning of Runway 30.

—Okay, KLM, 80, ah, correction, 4805, taxi straight ahead, ah, for the runway and make a backtrack.

—Roger, make a backtrack. KLM 4805 is now on the runway.

—4805, roger.

—Approach, you want us to turn left at Charlie 1, taxiway Charlie 1?

—Negative, negative, taxi straight ahead, ah, up to the end of the runway and make backtrack.

—Okay, sir.

* * *

Grubbs watches the KLM proceed ahead and waits for his taxi instructions from the tower.

When they arrive, they are not entirely welcome. The controllers instruct him to travel down the runway and exit it using one of the transverse taxiways. This will clear the path for KLM 4805 to take off.

The directive leaves Grubbs with a vague feeling of discomfort. Instinctively, he would prefer to hold at the entry to the runway until KLM has taken off. He just isn't entirely sold on the idea of creeping up the runway behind KLM. Two planes on the runway at the same time is never a great thing.

—We could hold here, if that's alright? he says to Bragg, who is responsible for radio communications with the tower.

Bragg is distracted by his airport map and his conversation with the tower. He doesn't hear the captain.

The moment has passed. The men have their instructions. They will comply.

But they are having their own issues getting to grips with what it is exactly that they are supposed to be doing.

The controllers have instructed them to travel down the runway and exit it using one of the transverse taxiways. This will clear the path for KLM 4805 to take off. The question is, which taxiway?

Bragg radios the tower:

—Ah, we were instructed to contact you and also to taxi down the runway, is that correct?

—Affirmative, taxi into the runway and, ah, leave the runway third, third to your left.

—Third to the left, okay.

Grubbs motors into the runway and starts inching along behind KLM, ahead in the distance. But, like Van Zanten, he finds the controller's accent a little hard to understand. He and Bragg start having a little dispute about which taxiway the controller means them to turn into.

—I think he said first, Grubbs says.

—I'll ask him again.

There are two sources of confusion here. One is Azcunaga's accent. Another is that the Pan American crew are unsure where he is counting from when he says "third". This is because they have already passed Charlie taxiway one. So does he mean "first", that is the next turn off; or does he mean Charlie taxiway 3; or does he mean the third exit from where they are positioned, which is in fact Charlie taxiway four?

Conveniently, their map does not designate the taxiways by number, nor are the turn offs marked on the actual runway. All they have to go off is the controller's instructions, and however they can best interpret those instructions.

* * *

And then, almost as if summoned by an unseen hand of evil, they come: the clouds.

Rolling down the mountains, they descend on the airport with a peculiar air of inevitability. And in a matter of moments, what had been a bright, clear afternoon becomes dim, damp and dark. The runway and all its craft are enveloped the thickest of fog; the kind where you can barely see your own arm stretched out in front of you.

Robert Bragg later described something almost paranormally surreal about this bank of cloud.

We noticed that this fog bank basically came off of the south mountain range and as we were taxiing down the fog bank was very obvious, it was coming down off the sides of the mountain, and it was weird looking because it came down and stopped right on the runway. It didn't go past the runway. It just stopped right on the runway.

* * *

Bragg, scanning the mysterious, murky world from the cockpit windows, is frustrated at this, yet another, obstacle being hurled in their path.

Not just frustrated; that doesn't quite cover it. Anxious too. His next words, delivered in his characteristically understated tones, nonetheless signify the flowering of alarm:

—Well, I don't think they have takeoff minimums anywhere right now.

Takeoff minimums in aviation lexicon refer to the minimum level of visibility stipulated by regulations to permit safe takeoff of aircraft. He is referring, of course, to the minimums he has learned during his commercial training back home in the United States. Right now they are in Spanish territory. Who knows what the Spanish minimums are, but Bragg is pretty sure this is well below what is acceptable.

What he is really saying is that unless visibility quickly improves, neither they, nor KLM, should be attempting to take off at all.

All of this leaves aside the fact that, as things stand, they are completely lost on the runway.

As if things can't get any worse, now the voice of Fernando Azcunaga delivers some more bad news.

—Gentlemen, be advised that the runway centerline lights are out of service.

Bragg glances at Grubbs, shaking his head. He flips over his departure and approach chart. This is a chart produced by his employer, Pan Am, which stipulates runway takeoff minimums with and without lighting. It states the FAA regulation that where centerline lights are out, 700 meters is the minimum required visibility.

And without centerline lights, not only do they not have the minimums to takeoff, they have even less hope of identifying the correct taxiway.

What was before a matter of confusion about the controller's directions has now degenerated into difficulty even detecting with their eyes the turnoffs.

To give them the best chance to make out where they need to turn, Grubbs is moving the *Clipper* along the runway at a glacial pace. Bragg is glancing back and forth between his airport map and what he can see of the sides of the runway, trying to make out the correct turn.

By looking at the map, they can see that Charlie taxiway 3 is the first available exit that will take them to the clear portion of the major parallel taxiway, and off the active runway.

But there is a problem: the taxiway is angled in such a way that they cannot get into it. It is a narrow taxiway angled back in the direction of the parking apron, the opposite direction to that which they should be travelling. They will have to make a sharp turn to get into it, and then another sharp turn at the end of it to get onto the main taxiway, if they are to be facing the right direction: that is, towards the holding point for runway 30.

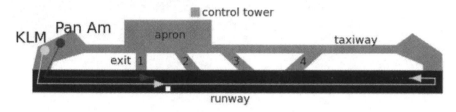

A smaller plane could manage it easily; but not a jumbo.

Surely this *can't* be the exit the controller means.

Bragg muses aloud about the problematic angles of taxiway 3.

—The first one is a ninety-degree turn [by "first" he means the next turn available to them, which is fact taxiway 3].

—Yeah, okay.

—Must be the one after. I'll ask him again.

Grubbs thinks maybe they could make the angles on the turn, with some difficulty.

—Okay. We could probably go in, it's ah ...

Bragg is less confident:

—You gotta make a ninety-degree turn!

—Yeah, uh ...

—Ninety-degree turn to get around this ... this one down here it's a forty-five.

Charlie taxiway 4 is a reasonable 45 degree turn that will have them facing the correct direction to travel from the main taxiway to the holding point for the runway.

Surely that's the one the tower means.

They decide to make one last ditch effort to confirm their instructions.

The portion of transcript below shows the process by which they arrive at a conclusion which is fact wrong.

—Would you confirm that you want the *Clipper* one seven three six to turn left at the third intersection?

—The third one, sir, one, two, three, third, third one.

—One, two, that makes it four.

—Good. That's what we need right, the third one.

Now Warns, trying to be lighthearted, interposes some little pep talk.

—We'll make it yet!

The crew go through the remainder of their taxi checklist. The transcript then resumes as follows:

—That's two (Grubbs, counting off the taxiways as they pass them).

—Yeah, that's 45 [degrees] there (Warns).

—Yeah (Grubbs).

—That's this one right here (Bragg).

— Yeah, I know (Grubbs).

—Okay. Next one is almost a 45, huh, yeah (Warns).

—But it goes …Yeah, but it goes … ahead, I think (it's) gonna put us on (the) taxiway (Grubbs).

—Yeah, just a little bit, yeah (Warns).

—Maybe he, maybe he counts these (are) three (Bragg).

—Huh? (Grubbs).

—Oh, I like this! (Warns, sarcastic).

For their part, the tower have made their own mistake. Taxiway 3 is indeed the appropriate taxiway to take; it is the first available that will lead *Clipper* to the open portion of the main taxiway, and off the runway. But a large plane can't navigate its angles.

Azcunaga is thinking in the way he is accustomed to; he is thinking about what a smaller plane, the kind that is usually on the ground at this airport, can capably do.

All other things being equal, the fact that Pan Am are lingering too long on the runway wouldn't ordinarily be too much cause for concern.

But all else is not equal.

Pan-Am aren't even contemplating, at this point, what is actually going on at the other end of the runway, where KLM is in fact getting ready for a premature departure.

Note that the tower had said visibility was down to 500 meters, Bragg later said. *We basically thought the airport was closed.*

As it turned out, KLM was in fact on the move. But why?

Chapter 3

The Final Moments

There's an old saying that there is three sides to every story; yours, theirs, and what really happened.

In this case there were four. The same set of circumstances were interpreted differently by our three groups of protagonists, the Pan Am crew, the KLM crew and the controllers. These misunderstandings were to prove devastating and fatal; but the truth about what really happened would not be known until well after the event.

* * *

Fernando Azcunaga is smack in the middle of one of the busiest and most stressful shifts of his life, coordinating departures for all the international carriers back to Las Palmas.

His shirt patched with perspiration, fatigued and yet pumped full of the adrenaline he needs to carry him through, he just keeps going, and now he can finally see the light at the end of the tunnel. So despite everything, he's actually feeling pretty good—that is, until the huge bank of fog settles on the runway. Now, his job is made that much more difficult again, because he can't make visual contact with the aircraft.

Right now his main concern is *Clipper*, because the crew seem to be having some difficulty locating their turn.

Dimly he is aware that he hasn't given KLM their ATC clearance yet, even though they are well on their way into their taxi to the end of the runway. The ATC clearance, distinct from the takeoff clearance, is simply a set of instructions for the route on which to proceed out of the airport once airborne.

It is normally issued to a crew before their taxi run so the pilots can be well prepared and have their flight path clearly established well before they are ready for takeoff.

He did radio KLM to give them their ATC clearance, in accordance with standard procedure. But KLM unexpectedly declined to receive it at the time. Azcunaga assumes they are busy with their taxi and pre-flight checklists and can't get to him.

It is not ideal to leave everything to the last moment in this fashion, but very well. He continues his work and waits for KLM to return his call in their own time.

At just after 5:00 pm, Azcunaga receives the call from the *Rhine*. First Officer Klaas Meurs is heard on the radio:

—Uh, the KLM four eight zero five is now ready for takeoff ... uh, and we're waiting for our ATC clearance.

Azcunaga can't see KLM but he takes it that they are holding at the end of the runway waiting to depart. He relays their ATC clearance as requested.

—KLM eight seven zero five, uh, you are cleared to the Papa beacon climb to and maintain flight level nine zero right turn after takeoff proceed with heading zero four zero until intercepting the three two five radial from Las Palmas VOR.

—Ah roger, sir, replies Meurs. We're cleared to the Papa beacon flight level nine zero, right turn out zero four zero until intercepting the three-two-five and we're now, uh, at takeoff.

—Okay, says Azcunaga, and pauses momentarily, trying to formulate his response.

The source of his hesitation is Meurs' ambiguously phrased read back: "We are now, uh, at takeoff."

Given that Azcunaga hasn't yet read them their takeoff clearance, he assumes Meurs means that they are in takeoff position, and will be awaiting their clearance. But the wording of the read back is non-standard enough to get his attention.

The cogs of his mind quickly whirring, Azcunaga suddenly intuits that KLM seem to be in a real hurry, and it is possible that they have assumed the ATC clearance, coming at the time it does, is also a clearance to take-off. Azcunaga quickly finishes his sentence in an effort to correct any such assumption:

—Standby for takeoff. I will call you.

At this same moment, a transmission arrives from Pan Am. The crew have heard Meurs over the radio, and they too are sufficiently alarmed to offer their own correction:

—And we're still on the runway, the *Clipper* one-seven-three-six!

Azcunaga hears nothing further from KLM, which he takes as a tacit acceptance of his instruction to wait.

He then asks Pan Am to advise when they have turned off onto the taxiway, so he will be ready to send KLM on their way.

—Roger Alpha one seven three six report when clear.

—Ok, replies Bragg. We'll report when clear.

With the finalization of this exchange, Azcunaga now feels the situation is well in hand, and confidently moves onto other tasks.

* * *

Let us now replay these same moments from the perspective of the Pan Am crew.

At the time that Meurs radios the tower for KLM's ATC clearance, they are moving slowly along the runway towards exit C4, having missed their assigned turn onto C3. When they hear Meurs speaking on the radio, they know that KLM are positioned at the end of the runway ready to takeoff, but like Azcunaga, they certainly aren't thinking they are yet on the move, given they haven't been issued their final clearance.

But Bragg and Grubbs feel a slight jolt of panic at Meurs' peculiar read back of the ATC clearance, the same one that set alarm bells ringing for Azcunaga: "we are now, uh, at takeoff".

—No, eh! says Grubbs.

—And we are still taxiing down the runway, Bragg quickly interposes over the radio. The *Clipper* one-seven-three-six!

Once the crew hear Azcunaga instructing KLM to stand by for takeoff and wait for his call, they relax a little. They are further heartened when Azcunaga radios and asks them to confirm when they are clear of the runway.

All is well—everybody is now on the same page.

The passengers in the cabin are contentedly thinking they are about to leave Los Rodeos and join their cruise liner for the holiday of a lifetime. And the crew are now imagining, with a sense of relief, that they have clarified their position with KLM and the tower.

This feeling of relief is reinforced by the fact that by this time, they are in the process of getting off the runway, having started their turn onto C4, the exit they have erroneously decided is the one meant for them.

The following exchange suggests a renewed atmosphere of joviality in the *Clipper* cockpit. The men even take a light-hearted poke at the captain of the *Rhine*.

Even so, the jibe is laced with a suggestion that the team are not entirely confident they are yet out of the woods.

—Let's get the hell out of here…

—Yeah, he's anxious isn't he?

—Yeah, after he held us up for half an hour. Now he's in a rush!

* * *

It is perfectly understandable that the controllers and the Pan Am crew were feeling reassured after this exchange between our protagonists. It seems almost inconceivable, after that, that there could have been any misunderstanding.

But this is a tragedy in which the inconceivable is to play a leading role.

To begin with, while Captain Jacob Van Zanten is backtracking down the runway to the far end where he will make his 180-degree turn to get into position for takeoff, he has a number of things on his mind other than the immediate technical and logistical details with which he is faced. It is for this reason that he declines to receive the ATC clearance at the time Azcunaga initially offers it. He and Meurs are indeed pre-occupied with their taxi and pre-flight checklists. But Van Zanten is still also worried about time.

He is relieved to hear that his duty limit gives him several clear hours, until half-past six, to get to Las Palmas, drop off his passengers, and return to Amsterdam.

He thinks he can make it. He can make this happen. It will be alright.

But now, he is observing with alarm the same bank of cloud that descended onto the runway and so spooked our friends in the cockpit of the *Clipper*.

This adds a degree of urgency to his situation once again. Because if he doesn't get off the ground soon, he will be trapped on Tenerife after all. He will not have the visibility minimums for takeoff.

Having completed his turn at the end of the runway, the captain begins advancing the throttles of the engines.

The meaning of this gesture is not entirely clear; is he getting ready to go now, or is he just warming up for his takeoff roll?

Either way, it is enough to give First Officer Klaas Meurs pause.

—Wait a minute, Meurs says, we don't have an ATC clearance.

Meurs refers here to the clearance for headings once airborne. The takeoff clearance, as we have established, is another matter altogether. They haven't received that either.

Van Zanten's response smacks slightly at indignation at an inferior questioning his authority:

—No, I know that. Go ahead, ask.

Meurs radios the tower:

— Uh, the KLM 4805 is now ready for takeoff and we're waiting for our ATC clearance.

—Uh, you are cleared to the Papa beacon. Climb to and maintain flight level 90 … right turn after takeoff proceed with heading 040 until intercepting the 325 radial from Las Palmas VOR.

Here, the tower have given the ATC clearance, which the captain apparently confuses for an ATC and takeoff clearance rolled into one, given its timing now that he is in position at the end of the runway.

He advances the throttles again.

Meurs notes this as an indication that Van Zanten wants to start the roll. He knows they haven't been given takeoff clearance. But he is loath to correct his captain a second time.

And this is the source of his strangely worded confirmation to the tower:

—Ah, roger, sir, we're cleared to the Papa beacon flight level 90, right turn out 040 until intercepting the 325 … and we're now, uh, at takeoff.

Meurs' read back combines confirmation of the ATC clearance with confirmation of a takeoff clearance which has never been issued.

Now, Azcunaga—no doubt confused by Meur's wording, and taking the more optimistic interpretation of his meaning—responds in the affirmative:

—Okay.

Following this, the KLM crew hear a pause followed by a three second high-pitched static squeal.

This sound, known in aviation lexicon as a heterodyne, is caused by simultaneous transmissions over radio. In this particular instance, the overlapping transmissions are Azcunaga's instruction to KLM to stand by and wait for his call to receive their takeoff clearance, and Robert Bragg's urgent message that Pan Am is still on the runway.

Because the transmissions overlap and cancel each other out, the KLM crew hear neither message.

Normally, flights communicate with air traffic control ATC via two-way VHF radios. The pilot or controller clicks the microphone, speaks and waits for an acknowledgment or "readback." It differs from talking on the telephone in that only one party can speak at a time. The difficulty occurs when two microphones are clicked at the same instant. The transmissions are effectively canceled out and instead, nothing will be heard but a screech of static or a high-pitched squeal. The pilots and controllers, however, do not realize the block has occurred.

Perhaps the sound of the heterodyne in itself should be enough to give Captain Van Zanten cause for worry. After all, it might lead him to conclude that there was some message possibly meant for him, that he did not hear.

Either way, he activates the thrust levers and starts to roll.

He isn't focused on the meaning of the heterodyne. He is focused on the one word he did hear Azcunaga say: "Okay". That's an affirmative. He has been given permission to takeoff.

And with that, the stage is set.

"We Gaan!" says Captain Van Zanten, releasing the brakes. "We're going!"

There is still one final opportunity to avert disaster. Captain Van Zanten doesn't notice it, and First Officer Meurs doesn't either, but the KLM flight engineer, Willem Schreuder, does. This is the tail part of a transmission between *Clipper* and the tower:

—Ah-Papa Alpha 1736 report runway clear.

—Okay, we'll report when we're clear.

—Thank you.

Schreuder bends forward in his chair, and tentatively enquires:

—Is he not clear then, that Pan American?

For whatever reason, Meurs and Van Zanten confidently shoot him down:

—Jawel! (Oh yes!) they both emphatically declare.

Meurs and Van Zanten are engrossed in the tasks associated with the takeoff roll. Possibly, because their attention is elsewhere, they don't hear the transmission; or, perhaps they do hear it, but assume the tower are talking to another aircraft, not Pan Am, because Azcunaga uncharacteristically refers to it as "Papa Alpha" instead of "Clipper", the name he has been using until that time.

Several seconds later, Meurs calls "V1", signifying that KLM has approached takeoff speed. It is now too late to stop.

Chapter 4

The Catastrophe

It is impossible to know what is going on in Van Zanten's mind in the remaining moments.

Perhaps he is simply pleased. Pleased, and reassured. His mission is accomplished. With a full load of fuel and a safe window of time remaining until his duty limit, he and his passengers are on their way back to Las Palmas.

Perhaps he has a vague intuition that something is wrong.

We just don't know.

What does seem likely is that the only individual in the KLM cockpit feeling a sense of abject terror at this moment, is Willem Schreuder, the man who tried to bring the impending catastrophe to the attention of his captain, and then meekly retreated in silence to await his certain and imminent death.

I have often felt such intense heartbreak for Schreuder in these last moments of his life. What a terrible, terrible thing. Silently turning away. Silently giving up. Knowing all the time what horror is just around the corner.

The passengers, on the other hand, have no idea anything is wrong. The moment about to arrive will be a brutal surprise for them all.

Van Zanten and Meurs are concentrating on the immediate objective of getting into the sky, their concentration and awareness fully focused on the mechanics of the task at hand. The Flight Engineer, however, has just finished his most active period of duty and is now sitting back. It is likely for this reason that he is the only one who notices the transmission alerting them of the fact that the Pan American is still on the runway.

The moment that Van Zanten grasps his mistake, and realizes that Schreuder is right, occurs some twelve seconds after Schreuder tries to warn him.

He has just begun rotation when he finally sights the Pan American ship slewing across the runway through the fog.

—Neuken! (Fuck!) he says.

Acting on sheer instinct—it is too late to do anything else—he pulls back hard on the control column, in hopes he can somehow get airborne and clear the Pan American.

But it is too premature, especially when carrying a full tank of fuel that greatly drags his speed. The *Rhine*'s tail strikes hard on the runway, sending up a shoal of sparks, further hindering his attempt to get airborne.

Van Zanten certainly makes a valiant effort. He tries with everything he has.

His nose succeeds in clearing the Pan American ship, but his landing gear crashes through the upper deck. The impact tears out KLM's hydraulic lines, and along with them, all its control surfaces.

Now this plane simply can't fly.

It limps through the air a few more seconds before collapsing onto the runway, and sliding another 150 or so meters before coming to rest. What was the pride of the Dutch is now a sad, twisted hunk of wreckage, lying prone with its engines torn off.

The full load of fuel which the captain, with such seeming foresight, took into his tanks instantly ignites and what is left of the *Rhine* is immediately enveloped in a massive, fearsome ball of fire.

All aboard are incinerated within moments.

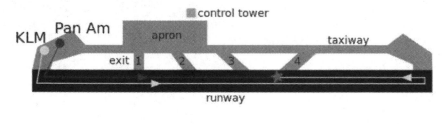

* * *

Let us replay these moments from the other perspective, that of the Clipper and its crew and passengers.

Some of them will live to tell. And it really is a story unlike anything you've ever heard.

At the moment that the *Rhine* is hurtling towards them through the fog, Grubbs, Bragg and Warns aren't contemplating that anything like what is about to take place could truly be happening. Bragg later explained:

When we first saw the KLM airplane, it didn't surprise us too much, because we were aware that he was down there. And the first thing that got my attention was that his landing lights were on, and that's one of the very last things that a pilot does when you receive the takeoff clearance ... then it was very obvious that the airplane was moving, coming at us, and my initial reaction was, I said very loudly, "I think he's moving!"

At this moment, Grubbs pushes the levers to full power, turning his ship 27 degrees to get off the runway.

—There he is! Look at him! Goddamn that son-of-a-bitch is coming!

—Get off! Get off! Get off!

It is too late. Bragg turns and looks out of his right-side window to see the KLM rotating and lifting off the ground, the red rotating beacon on the belly of the fuselage looming towards them.

He is a realist, used to taking the most absurd incidents in stride with bland equanimity. But this is the first time in his life he has beheld a thing, and been literally unable to comprehend that it is happening.

There is nothing left to do but duck. And duck he does.

A desperate measure, unlikely to secure survival. But much to his surprise, at the moment of impact, all he hears is a gentle "clunk".

It was a very slight noise ... so minor it was unbelievable.

He opens his eyes. What is this? He surveys his body, his arms and legs—look, they are still attached to his trunk!

Establishing he is in one piece, he stands up. His captain, Grubbs, there he is also: an integrated, whole human. Not even a scratch or scrape.

Miraculously, they have been spared. Maybe things aren't that bad!

But then, he looks around.

All the cockpit windows are gone.

To the left, the lounge, and all 28 people who had been seated there—gone.

The right wing is on fire. The engines are still running, posing an unacceptable risk of further fire and explosion. Bragg reaches down to grab the four start up levers. Nothing happens—all the plane's control lines have been severed.

He raises his hand to pull the fire engine shutoff levers—and there is nothing there.

The entire upper deck of the cabin has been shorn off by KLM's belly and landing gear. And with it, the roof of the cockpit, where several key controls are located, is gone.

The men are perched atop an exposed promontory like a pair of lonely seagulls.

There was just a void, just a big hole and I could see all the way to the tail of the airplane. It was like someone had taken a big knife and just sliced the top of the airplane off.

Moments later the flight deck floor, together with that of the wrecked upper deck, collapses, spilling the burning bodies of passengers from the upper deck lounge into the main deck cabin below. About now, Bragg starts thinking it's time to get out of this plane.

And as before I had said "get off!" to the captain, this time I was saying "get out, get out!"

Where they stand, there is only about a foot of floor left. The rest is a gaping hole. Thinking nothing of the distance to the ground—some thirty-eight feet—Grubbs and Bragg leap through this hole and out of the airplane.

Warns' whereabouts are unknown. Grubbs and Bragg don't yet know it, but he too has survived; after the impact he finds himself dangling from the roof of the first-class cabin beneath the cockpit. He too escapes through the hole in the cabin floor.

Bragg is lucky—he emerges from his immediate ordeal with nothing more than a sprained ankle. Grubbs sustains burns to his hands and arms while escaping the flaming aircraft.

Little do they know as yet that many of the passengers have similarly discovered that leaping to the ground from cabin deck level is the only way out. Many will sustain much more severe injuries than they do.

* * *

Spare a thought for these passengers in the Pan American cabin, who—unlike the flight crew—had no clue whatsoever of any lingering threat posed by the harried Captain of another Boeing 747 down at the end of the runway.

The first they knew of any trouble was when KLM slammed into them, tearing the entire roof of the cabin off.

The upper deck, where nearly thirty passengers are seated, is immediately torn away in the impact. Most of these people die instantly. A lucky few, injured but alive, spill down into the cockpit and first-class cabin below. They will make their way to the ground by the same route Grubbs and Bragg took—through the hole in the fuselage that leads there via a drop of nearly forty feet.

Once they escape the plane, their torment is far from over.

Legs and ankles snap like twigs on the hard surface of the tarmac after a fall from such a height. These survivors' best bet, if they want to live, is to somehow drag themselves to safety on their hands and knees.

Arms, elbows and knees scrape against the bitumen. Hair and clothing is on fire. Hair and clothing, melting into the skin with the heat of a thousand suns. Jet fuel spilling onto the runway, burning and abrading the open wounds.

Those passengers inside the cabin who have survived the initial impact—most on the starboard side, where KLM hit, are killed outright—are barely able to process what is happening, and have precious little time to escape.

Let us contemplate the words of one survivor of a plane crash who tried to give an answer to the question, "what is it like"?

Chaos. Confusion. Everything flying around everywhere. You realize all this time you were actually inside a beer can. It's just little bits of aluminum between you and whatever you hit.

A structure that had seemed so strong and sturdy is now swirling in pieces around you. There is spilled luggage, unidentifiable wires and twisted bits of fuselage everywhere. You can't even see what or where anything is. The air fills with particles and smoke from the fire. Everything is moving—matter and people. The people scramble and scream around you. You wish they'd stop screaming—it's a terrible sound—but you're screaming too!

Joan Jackson is a flight attendant on the *Clipper* who, along with her colleague, Suzanne Donovan, has survived the initial crash.

The first thing was this huge loud noise. And the only thing I could liken it to is as if each molecule of air exploded. It was just that loud.

The fire comes immediately from the starboard side, where the impact has occurred. This raging fire rapidly engulfs the starboard wing and that entire side of the fuselage. Seats, luggage and human bodies are alight. Smoke fills the cabin, making it hard to breathe.

I opened my eyes and looked at the cabin. Everything was on fire.

Those who can, scramble through the aisles and over seats to the port-side wing area. Here, an emergency exit and another gaping hole in the fuselage offers an escape point.

There seems to be two kinds of passenger, two kinds of reaction. Those who take a chance and leap to action, knowing time is short—and those who simply sit, stymied and shocked, tethered to their chairs.

Floy Olson, a resident at Leisure World retirement village in Laguna Hills, hears her husband Paul Peck cry out, "Floy, unfasten your seat belt! Let's get out!" Leaping from her chair, she glances over and sees her friend Lorraine Larsen, also a resident at Leisure World, just sitting there like a zombie with her mouth open. Lorraine and her husband Karl will both perish in the fire.

The passengers step out onto the wing where, again, they must drop some forty feet to get to the ground. The wing is soon covered with some 45 to 50 passengers. These people, a small handful who escape via an emergency exit at the far rear of the plane, and those—like Grubbs and Bragg—who drop to the ground through the hole near the nose of the plane, are the sole survivors on the *Clipper*.

The rest of the passengers are either overcome by smoke and flames, or prevented from reaching the exits by collapsed, burning fuselage. They are doomed to die in the final conflagration.

The total evacuation time for the survivors is less than one minute.

The plane's engines are still running at full tilt. Eventually they begin to disintegrate, scattering scalding debris in all directions. Having survived the initial crash, anyone who drops from the wing in the vicinity of an engine is likely to die in the most painful and terrifying way, assailed by a hail of burning metal shard.

This is in fact is the terrible fate of one flight attendant who initially survives.

Another woman, terrified of the long jump off the wing, makes the unfortunate decision to slide down the side of an engine instead, and sustains third degree burns all over the back of her body.

Passengers are seen leaping from the wing, their clothes and hair on fire.

These souls are rewarded for their bravery with broken bones and massive grazes.

Robert Bragg later relayed a searing account of one of the unluckiest of these folk.

I saw a man pulling a lady by the ankle and running as fast as he could. It was strange. I asked myself, why is he doing it that way?! Well, this was his wife and when she jumped, she was one of the first jumpers and everybody hit on top of her and it broke both arms, both legs and her back ... but he accomplished what he wanted to do. He got her away from the airplane.

When the rescue teams finally arrive, they are greeted by the sight of elderly, vulnerable people crawling in desperation from the flaming wreckage and jet fuel with broken bodies, severe burns and charred clothing.

Bragg wanders amongst the survivors, doing what he can to offer aid and comfort, but is left with the distinct impression his efforts fall short. What can anyone really say or do?

He stumbles across a woman with severe burns to her arms and back, blackened clothing ripped to shreds, and singed hair patched with reddened, bare scalp.

I said, everything would be okay. It was the only thing I could think to say ... and she just collapsed.

A rescue worker comes across the charred, lifeless bodies of a mother and child.

You could still see the gesture of the mother, embracing and trying in vain to protect her kid.

Victor Grubbs, having reached a safe distance from the plane, stands surveying the scene with utter disbelief. Barely anything recognizable remains of his beautiful plane, and he knows that any of his passengers still trapped inside are doomed. His face bloodied, his burned arms hanging limp and helpless at his sides, he is dazed beyond word or action.

In the grim finale, the center fuel tank explodes and shoots a flame a couple hundred feet high into the air. Now the entire fuselage, but for the port-side wing, is engulfed in flames and collapses in on itself. All trapped within still breathing are burned alive.

At last, the screaming stops. It is replaced by an eerie silence: the silence of death.

The survivors of the Tenerife disaster are left to fend for themselves for a ghastly twenty minutes before help arrives. Once the rescue teams are on site, there is nothing left for them to do but tend to the injured. There is nobody left to save.

Jack Ridout, a survivor from Alpine California, wandered shell-shocked through the scene of devastation, the torturous memory from a few moments earlier of the faces of his fellow passengers staring blankly ahead, still strapped in their seats and too shocked to move.

I've never seen so many dead bodies. There was nothing. Nothing but burning gasoline and metal.

Chapter 5

The Aftermath

The slow response of the fire and emergency crews could not be blamed on the authorities at Los Rodeos. Instead it was the consequence of a similar train of mishaps and misunderstandings that caused the catastrophe in the first place.

That sinister pall of fog largely responsible for the collision was also dense enough to cloak the massive blazes that were all that remained of *Rhine* and *Clipper*. Azcunaga had heard the explosions, but was uncertain of their source. Due to the low visibility, he was unable to determine the location of the wreckage, or even that a serious airplane accident had occurred. Instead, he thought a bomb had exploded at the airport, possibly related to the terrorist attack at Las Palmas.

A crash on his own turf is every controller's worst nightmare. The men were understandably reluctant to immediately embrace the most unpleasant explanation for what they had heard.

Suspicions naturally grew when their efforts to contact the *Clipper* and KLM met with no response.

Clipper had tried to contact the tower for help, but because the control lines of the Pan Am had been severed in the impact, they had no working radio. As for KLM, they could hardly reply—they were all dead.

* * *

The crew of a jet parked on the apron made out a distant orange glow through the soupy grey. They sent an immediate transmission to the tower alerting them of a suspected fire, although they were unable to describe the location.

The blaze from the wreckage of the KLM was also spotted and reported by the pilot of a plane circling in a holding pattern above the terminal.

The controllers immediately sounded the fire alarm and instructed their trucks to be ready for a quick departure as soon as the position of the fire could be established. But still, they were unaware that there were not just one, but two blazes they needed to attend to.

An airport workman rushed back to the fire station and reported that there was a fire "to the left of the aircraft parking area."

The fire he had seen was from the wreckage of KLM, so that way the trucks hurried forth. But all had perished on the *Rhine*, and where they really needed to get to was the site of the Pan Am wreckage, where survivors still desperately needed assistance.

The trucks were further delayed by the congestion on the parking apron. Navigating an obstacle course of parked planes, they eventually made out a glow through the fog. It radiated an intense heat that burned hotter with every meter to their destination, and when they arrived they saw a large aircraft, unmistakably a jumbo, completely consumed in fire but for the rudder and fin.

The heavy load of fresh fuel that Captain Jacob Van Zanten had fed into the *Rhine*'s tanks at Los Rodeos played a critical role in both the cause of the disaster—because it delayed both KLM and Pan Am to a point where visibility had drastically worsened—and its severity. In years to come aviation enthusiasts would speculate about whether, had he been lighter in weight, he could have managed to safely clear the Pan Am, and leapfrog over it into the air as he hoped; or whether, had there been less fuel on board, there might have at least been some survivors.

As it stood, there was no question at all in the minds of the fire service and rescue team, as soon as they arrived, that not one life has been spared.

Diligently they began the herculean task of putting out the fire, dumping massive amounts of fire-retardant foam on the wreckage. The job would take them all night.

But a short time after they began, the fog slowly started to clear. And then, they saw it—another red glow in the distance.

From where they stood, it wasn't much to look at. If there was any doubt that the staff of Los Rodeos were entirely unprepared for the scale of this tragedy, here was more confirmation: they at first assumed that it was simply a detached flaming piece of wreckage from the same aircraft.

On approaching they were thoroughly corrected. Here was another great jumbo, burning intensely, the final survivors straggling away from the wreckage.

All the fire vehicles now concentrated their efforts on this second aircraft, as the first was completely beyond saving. They arrived in time to stop the port wing of the Pan Am being completely consumed by the fire, and this was a good outcome being that between 15 and 20 tons of fuel were subsequently recovered from it; their actions thus prevented a more devastating and dangerous final conflagration.

But they were much too late to save those still trapped inside the plane.

For the survivors, the late arrival of help—even if they came to understand the reasons later—left them feeling desperate and helpless.

No one came down to our site and that was one of the things I was wondering about, Bragg later said. *Why in the world hadn't anyone come down to our plane and help us.*

* * *

It so happened that some residents who lived near the airport noticed the flames from Pan Am well before the fire and rescue service did.

Surviving crew members had spent the better part of twenty minutes trying to round up the passengers and get them away from the burning plane. Looking around they were perplexed to see some stragglers still standing around in the path of danger. It then dawned on them that these were not passengers, but civilians. Boldly, they had climbed over the perimeter fences and rushed to the site to assist those lucky few who had not yet perished to escape the grave threat still posed by fuel and fire.

With no resources other than their own bodies, bravery and ingenuity they picked the survivors up, hoisted them on their backs and carried them to safety. When one lot of passengers were deposited at a safe distance, back they went to grab another load.

The challenges that faced the people of Tenerife in coming to grips with this catastrophe were not due to any defects of their nature. There was no incompetence, callousness or failure of will in their conduct; only a terrible struggle to face, with limited resources, a situation for which they could never have been prepared. In truth the only thing of beauty that emerged at the end of that horrendous afternoon was the selfless charity and inventiveness shown by those who would, and did, do anything to help, no matter how desperate and seemingly futile were the circumstances.

It was this same disarming streak of kindness and sheer tenacity that prompted the officials of Los Rodeos to call a fleet of taxicabs, have them drive into the terminal and straight to the accident site to retrieve the burned and injured and take them to one of the two hospitals on the island. The taxicabs could get there faster than the ambulances could, and there were insufficient numbers of the latter. This was a tourist island, with a small residential population. The need for such large-scale medical services was unanticipated, but there were always plenty of cabs!

Survivors were momentarily disoriented by the surreal appearance of the sleek black sedans chauffeured by well-turned out men in suits and caps, as if—after all the insanity that had just unfolded—they were bound for no more than a pleasant holiday after all.

Good day Sir! Everything is under control, they would say, opening the rear door and bodily depositing the wounded in the back of the vehicle before departing at breakneck speed for the few available medical facilities.

Their determination was unmatched but even so, the drivers of the taxis and ambulances met with critical delays in carrying their charges to help and safety. Many roads were congested with the vehicles of civilians who, compelled by morbid curiosity, drove to the airport to get a closer look.

With the scale of the disaster now abundantly clear, officials moved swiftly. The governor of Tenerife, Antonio Oyarzabal, declared a state of emergency and at once ordered all operations at the airport suspended indefinitely.

The main runway was unusable, littered with debris and wreckage, with a massive gouge ripped out of it by the KLM tail strike.

Radio stations on the island issued emergency calls for all doctors and nurses to report to their stations, and within half an hour of the disaster all the medical personnel on Tenerife were on active duty. Vincent Pedraza, medical director of the Hospital General y Clinico which overlooked Tenerife Harbor, said the first injured began arriving at 5:30 pm. By six o'clock in the evening almost two hundred local residents voluntarily arrived at the hospitals to donate blood.

The hospitals, unused to such a large influx of patients—many suffering extremely serious burns—bustled with barely controlled chaos. The initial tally of survivors from the Pan American ship was seventy, but in the hours to follow nine of those lost their fight for life, so horrifically injured were they that their bodies could not sustain.

Bragg fortuitously located his crew mates Victor Grubbs, George Warns and four Pan Am flight attendants at the same hospital where he was brought for treatment of his comparatively minor injuries. Bragg had suffered only a sprained ankle in leaping from the burning plane. Being that he was fit and well, he decided to take charge of the task of making a count of the surviving Pan Am employees and immediately informing the airline.

I called Pan Am and I said this is Robert Bragg, I was the copilot on the Clipper 1276 and I want to give you some information about this accident and also give you the names of some people that I know survived and their comment was: what accident?

Much to Bragg's surprise, the first Pan American World Airways knew of the tragedy was his phone call.

What happened? They asked him.

Well, uh, a KLM jumbo took off without clearance and collided with us on the runway.

Thanks to Bragg, the airline were able to get immediate word to the loved ones of the crew members that despite a catastrophic accident on Tenerife, they were alive and, for the most part, well.

None who received such reassurances could have appreciated just how lucky the survivors were, until, during an emergency broadcast interrupting the national screening of a football game, the American people were informed for the first time of just what had happened on the idyllic island across the Atlantic.

The awe-inspiring Boeing 747 had been rolled out with much pride and fanfare just years earlier. Amidst all the excitement nobody wanted to give much thought to the possible downsides of such a large aircraft, capable of carrying so many passengers, should an accident occur. But some in commercial aviation were quietly troubled by the question: just what would happen if two of these beasts smashed into each other?

Well, here it was. Here was the very devastating answer to that question. More than 580 people dead: all aboard the Dutch aircraft, and all but a handful of survivors on the Pan Am. The first major accident in which the Boeing jumbo had been involved had turned out to be the deadliest aviation disaster in history.

If news of the catastrophe had been greeted with surprise by the Americans, the Dutch were equally—if not more—taken unawares. KLM's first response upon hearing what had happened was to immediately call for Jacob Van Zanten, as Head of Safety at KLM, to be deployed to Tenerife to head a team of accident investigators, not realizing that not only had he perished on board, but that he was the man whose actions would ultimately be held responsible for the disaster.

Such was the carrier's pride and confidence in Van Zanten that their first assumption was that he could not have been at fault.

* * *

5,000 kilos of foam (Tutogene) and 500,000 litres of water were needed to finally put out the fire of the wreckage. All night, while firefighters worked to extinguish the flames, efforts were also underway to find a solution for another pressing problem: what to do with all the bodies, many of which were so horrendously scorched they couldn't even be identified. Efforts to retrieve them from the wreckage continued through the nights of 27 and 28 March. In some cases bodies were not intact and sadly amongst the findings in the large debris fields around the crash sites where luggage, toys and bits of clothing had scattered, were charred lumps of unidentifiable human remains.

As unprepared as Los Rodeos was for the disaster they were equally unprepared for the task of managing and processing such a large number of dead. Initially, the blackened corpses were simply laid side by side in queues by the side of the runway. There, the smell of smoke and burnt flesh rising off the ground lingered for a matter of days.

Eventually, a makeshift morgue was erected in a large aircraft hangar. Over the next days row after row of wood coffins gradually filled the entire floor of the 2500 square meters building.

As there were insufficient caskets available on the island, Pan American flew more over from London into Tenerife. Peter Jennings, a correspondent for the BBC, went into the hangar and recorded footage of the enormous mass of wood coffins literally laid flush against one another in seemingly endless rows. This footage was later shown in television reports on the accident. The film itself is haunting, but probably does not capture the effect of seeing it up close and personal. Jennings later said it was the worst sight he had ever seen in his life.

That just gutted me ... just the sheer waste of it all ...

Ultimately all the coffins with their lifeless human contents were shipped to Holland and the United States by KLM and Pan Am respectively, depending on the identity of the deceased and where they had come from. Establishing that was no easy task.

As a Spanish official later confirmed in press reports, ninety-five percent of the bodies from both planes were burned beyond all recognition. The bodies, in many cases nothing more than shriveled carbaceous masses, were placed in bags and, separated by carrier, stored in a nearby hangar. Those in better condition were placed on makeshift beds in readiness for identification teams.

The condition of the bodies from the KLM plane in fact made it impossible to perform autopsies. The Spanish Justice Department in cooperation with the Dutch authorities agreed to have pathologists brought to Tenerife from Holland to assist with the task of sorting and identifying the dead. Members of the RIT (Dutch Emergency Identification Staff) arrived by helicopter from Las Palmas on 28 March to an odor of burning flesh they described as "terrible".

Spanish law required that the Dutch and American teams only began the process of identifying the dead after official permission was granted and within certain time limits. Because the American team arrived too late, they were denied permission, and all those victims had to be identified after the bodies were returned to the United States.

The Dutch team worked as fast as they could, but still could not make their deadline, thus many of the Dutch victims too would not be identified until they were returned to Holland. The RIT described a devastating scene in the hangar where the bodies were being temporarily stored. The smell was indescribable. The dead, once individuals possessed of unique attributes and personalities, lay in rows like items on an assembly line, all their dignity stripped away. Amongst them were toddlers and babies.

Because the American identification team had been denied permission to start work identifying the dead, their pathologists were not needed. They idled at the Hotel Mencey while waiting to be told if their assistance would be required, or alternatively, if they could return home.

One of them, Dr. William G. Eckert of Wichita, Kansas, told a group of listeners in the lobby that there should be no problem in identifying the corpses through the use of dental records and computers. "It's really a very small sample, 500 people," he said. "Two million facts can be spit out on a computer in minutes. This is modern technology at work."

A woman bystander retorted: "And modern technology got us into it."

* * *

Bodies were flown by Pan Am to Dover Air Force Base on 3 April, and on 4 April a team of experts began the somber task of identifying 326 American victims in a special mortuary. The Dutch papers reported on 8 April that that 108 victims from the KLM Boeing had been buried in a mass grave in Amsterdam.

The return of the dead to their countries of origin had to be effected speedily, because the Spanish officials informed the two airliners involved in the disaster that if they didn't evacuate the bodies from the island within forty-eight hours, they were going to dig a mass grave and simply bury them there. Understandably the Tenerife authorities could not reasonably accommodate the corpses for any sustained length of time in their facilities.

In the meantime flocks of journalists, investigators and other officials were descending on the island. A group of diplomats and military attaches from the United States Embassy in Madrid flew to Tenerife to give comfort and assistance to survivors. Because Los Rodeos was closed for any routine commercial traffic, the journalists had to come by ferry from Gran Canaria, a trip of three-and-a-half hours. Journalists native to the island clearly had an advantage on their overseas competitors and took full advantage; their photographs of the crash scenes were taken in the hours immediately following and were splashed all over the Spanish newspapers the following day.

Robert Bragg later said that these images in the Spanish papers were the first he knew of what had really happened to the KLM plane. *Spanish newspapers will put whatever they photograph on the front of the page*, he said drily. Bragg was referring to the confronting nature of the pictures, which unapologetically displayed burned victims piled on the ground. Aside from that, they clearly showed the extent of the wreckage of the *Rhine*—a barely recognizable hunk of twisted, charred metal—and listed the total death toll of the accident, at that point suspected to be over five hundred, but later confirmed as 583.

One survivor from the Pan Am jet demonstrated unusual resourcefulness and clarity of mind amidst all the chaos immediately following the accident, pulling out a camera and frantically snapping as many pictures as he could. Allegedly this man was later offered $50,000 for his photographs, but never saw a cent of the money. They appeared nonetheless in the *Time* magazine feature about the crash published on 11 April 1977.

Both Victor Grubbs and Robert Bragg were called upon to respond to a seemingly endless stream of requests for interviews during their hospital stays on Tenerife.

It happened about every ten minutes, they would come in and roll my single bed down to the telephone at the desk and it was another newspaper reporter. So finally I had to tell them, please do not come and roll me down the hall to speak to newspaper reporters. Just take their name and tell them we will get back to them. So that went on all night long.

Once discharged from the hospital, Bragg was installed temporarily in a hotel room near the airport under an anonymous name. This did little good, because as soon as he arrived he began receiving telephone calls from reporters. He was offered $50,000 for an exclusive article with the *National Enquirer*, which he declined; an article nonetheless appeared later in the publication with his name on it, despite his never agreeing to an interview or receiving any money. Grubbs was also offered $125,000 for an article, which he similarly turned down. Ethically and professionally the men felt bound to reject any such offers, given that the formal investigation had not yet had opportunity to arrive at its own conclusions.

That didn't really matter however as far as the press corps were concerned; what mattered to them was that this disaster, whilst undoubtedly a tragedy for the victims and their families, was also an unprecedented opportunity for them. The world certainly was not going to stop turning just because a few hundred people had died.

Amidst all the excitement, some wild stories and inaccuracies were circulating. One paper reported that a controller at Los Rodeos had hurled himself out of the tower to his death upon learning of the disaster. Some of Azcunaga's relatives had not yet heard from him, and flew into a panic.

That was a terrible week, Fernando later said with a heavy sigh.

Amongst those reading the reports of the disaster in the Spanish newspapers was Robina Van Lanschott. Overcome with shock and devastation, she realized that she has just escaped death by a hair's breadth … and that her friends Walter and Yvonne, and all the passengers she shared smiles and conversations with just days earlier, were gone.

Robina was saved by love. It was because she was in such a rush to see her boyfriend again that she decided not to get back on the plane. She is the sole survivor of the accident on the KLM aircraft.

* * *

Statistically, the majority of injuries and deaths in an air crash are caused by blunt force trauma sustained when bodies collide with matter: unmoored luggage, hurled objects, pieces of fuselage. This disaster was a little different, at least as far as the passengers on the Pan Am ship was concerned. The *Clipper* was moving at a slow rate when KLM collided with it. For those not killed in the initial impact, the principal threat therefore was fire.

The survivors knew this all too well. Their burning injuries were extensive and in many cases ultimately fatal. If the clothing a person is wearing catches fire, third-degree burns can develop in a matter of seconds. Some of those who escaped the plane alive had sustained burns to ninety percent of their bodies. Where burns to more than forty percent of the body occur, survival outcomes are very poor. Hence the initial number of survivors from the Pan Am—seventy—quickly dwindled to sixty-one.

The number one cause of death in severe burning injuries is in fact primary neurogenic shock. The shock is caused by pain so intense that the body shuts down altogether rather than allow the mind to be exposed to it.

If that initial hurdle is passed, fifty percent of those who die from burning injuries will do so within the next forty-eight hours, due to secondary shock—principally fluid loss from the burned skin surfaces. If a burn victim survives that threat, they may later go on to develop toxaemia from the absorption of poisonous metabolites from the burnt tissues, which can persist for several days, or sepsis.

Fluid loss from the burned skin can also cause secondary damage to the organs. Renal failure is often a consequence of severe burning injuries. Tissues that fail to regenerate may become necrotic and thus gangrene is also a possible outcome, with surgeries and amputations needed to spare the victim's life. Pulmonary oedema and damage to the bronchial system are also seen with the inhalation of smoke containing carbon monoxide and carbon dioxide, not to mention the toxic fumes that result when typical materials used in the construction and furnishing of aircraft are burned at high temperature.

The crew members from the Pan Am ship who had survived found it no easy matter to renounce the habit of checking in on the welfare of their passengers, and while this flight had already terminated days ago in the most horrible way, they continued to enquire after their charges while they lay languishing in their hospital beds.

Bragg was deeply affected by a number of these conversations. He and flight attendant Dorothy Kelly were the only crew survivors not seriously injured. They did rounds of the hospital checking on the patients.

It was bad in the respect that ... you'd be talking to someone very badly burned, and they would not realize how badly burned they were and you would leave their room and come back an hour later ... and they were passed away.

We might well ask, in just this type of situation, is it really better to survive than pass on? Should an individual survive severe burning injuries of the type that are sustained during an aviation disaster, they will usually have years of painful recovery and rehabilitation to look forward to, including multiple hospital stays for repeated skin grafts.

For the burn victims installed in hospitals on Tenerife their stay was to brief. The medical facilities on the island were nowhere near appropriate to the tasks that lay ahead in treating the survivors and helping them towards recovery. The medical personnel on the island were there to help the victims through those first critical hours and days; to give them the best chance simply to live. They were joined by a team of burns specialists flown in from the United States. Additionally an emergency hospital was opened at the United States Air Force Base at Torrejon, near Madrid, to help treat survivors if necessary.

On 29 March a United States Air-Force C-130 airplane evacuated fifty-six American survivors, many of whom were carried aboard on stretchers. These patients were being flown to specialist burn treatment centers at Brook Army hospital at San Antonio, Texas and the Cornell University Medical Centre, New York Hospital. Amongst them was Victor Grubbs, whose hands and arms were burned and bandaged. The C-130 travelled first to Las Palmas, where the survivors were transferred to a C-141 for a flight to McGuire Air Force base in New Jersey. On 30 March, two of these survivors died, one during the stop at Las Palmas and another en-route to the United States.

The C-141 arrived at McGuire Air Force base on 30 March, where the Burlington Emergency Medical Service were on hand to transport the injured survivors to Burlington County Memorial Hospital. Plans had to be abruptly altered however, as several patients were perilously close to death. They were taken instead in army ambulances to Walson Hospital at nearby Fort Dix. The head of the burns specialist unit at Fort Dix stated that there were eight seriously burned patients who were entering the most critical phases of their recovery, with the most acute danger presented by infection.

The C-141 plane continued to San Antonio where several crash victims were hospitalized in Brook Army Medical Centre. Colonel Pruitt, commander of the centre, said three patients were "seriously ill" and four others were "very seriously ill". On 18 April two more survivors died, bringing the death toll of the disaster at that time to 578 people.

Bragg himself left Tenerife on a small commuter plane, along with Peter Jennings, the BBC journalist, and eight surviving passengers who were, like himself, largely unharmed. They met a connecting Boeing 747 flight to London at Madrid via Las Palmas. This group thus had the surreal experience of passing through the airport for which they had originally been destined, but under radically different—and much more sorrowful—circumstances than those once imagined. Days earlier these passengers had been bound for Las Palmas to enjoy a dream vacation. Now all they could think was how much they wanted to get the hell out of there, and back home to the United States.

No matter their haste to return to the safe and welcoming arms of their loved ones, this cohort stepped onto the Pan American plane at Madrid with more than a flutter of unease. *I'll be the first to admit,* Bragg recalled, *it was an extremely strange feeling when we walked onto that Pan Am 747.* This was the first time they had been in a jumbo since the accident, and it was their only way home, but the otherwise unremarkable aircraft looked and felt exactly the same as the one that had nearly become their grave just a few days before. The trauma had abruptly returned to haunt them, just at the time when they were most desperate to forget.

Back on the archipelago, on 30 March the Roman Catholic bishop of Tenerife, Msgr. Luis Franco Gascon, led a moving ecumenical memorial service for the more than 570 who had already passed in the Cathedral of San Cristobal, in the town of La Laguna. The service was attended by a delegate of the Spanish King Juan Carlos I, along with a handful of survivors and their next of kin, airline officials and investigators. But perhaps surprisingly, the majestic sixteenth century church was filled primarily with Canary natives, who came in their hundreds to commemorate the dead and share in their families' outpouring of grief. This significant turn out from the islanders was perhaps not simply a testament to the good nature they had shown throughout the ordeal, but illustrated the fact that this terrible event was a tragedy not only for the nations represented in the incident, Holland and the United States, but for Canary peoples too.

It seemed a dark new day had dawned on the normally bright and tranquil islands, where the locals prided themselves on their hospitality to foreigners. Everywhere there was a sense that the place had been changed, perhaps irrevocably. The bishop began the memorial service with prayers for the souls of the dead, and went on to express that he and all Canary islanders shared the anguish of the victims' families.

He also spoke aloud the worries of many, observing the accident was likely to have severe repercussions for a nation whose economic lifeblood was tourism.

As it turned out, the commercial effect of the accident on the islands was to be mild and short-lived. As is so often the case with such monumental tragedies, somehow everyone simply picked themselves up and moved on.

As March came to a close the catastrophe, for all intents and purposes, was over: the officials had expressed their condolences, the runways, cleared of debris and repaired, were once again open for traffic, the living and the dead were returned to their homelands, and to the naked eye of an uninformed visitor it might well have appeared that nothing had ever happened at all on Tenerife.

Nonetheless, while on the surface all was once again business as usual, in fact the narrative of this disaster was entering its most critical phase, for it was now time to establish the truth of just how and why Pan Am and KLM had collided, and more importantly, call the actors to account for whatever their part may have been.

It goes without saying that, in an aviation accident like this, nobody wants to take the blame if it can be avoided—for wherever the blame is cast, is where the financial and reputational penalty also will accrue.

In theory the investigation process in aviation accidents is merely meant to contribute to understandings that will in future contribute to public safety. In reality it does impinge into the litigation process, since official findings are drawn upon in the resolution of claims.

In this particular case, the total anticipated for direct compensation claims was thought to be in the vicinity of $63 million dollars—and future settlements were likely to run to as much as $450 million, based on the estimates of the principal insurer, Lloyds of London.

Chapter 6

The Autopsy

The crash-resistant cockpit voice recorders were recovered intact and undamaged from both the Pan Am and KLM aircrafts on 29 March, and were immediately sent to Washington for transcription and analysis, along with the tower tapes containing records of the controllers' communications with both flight crews. This decision to send the tapes to Washington had been taken because the United States' investigative authority, the NTSB, were invited by the Spanish government to take an active role in the inquiry, along with Dutch investigative officials and representatives of KLM and Pan American World Airways.

While all this gives the impression of a desire for collaboration and even-handedness between the parties, and that impression is not entirely incorrect, it should not be overlooked that the nations and commercial entities concerned were very keen to defend their respective interests, which is made abundantly clear in the rather different findings represented in the official investigative reports prepared by the Spanish, American and Dutch authorities respectively.

As it was, in the early stages considerable confusion surrounded the circumstances of the collision. The possibility that deliberate sabotage, technical failures or unworthiness of craft had caused the accident was ruled out quickly, and human error of some sort was in the foreground of speculations from the beginning. The key questions surrounded the actions of the KLM crew, the Pan Am Crew and the controllers. It was not known whether KLM had been given clearance to take off, whether Pan Am had disobeyed or misunderstood their taxi instructions, or if the tower controllers had perhaps issued contra-dictory orders.

Notwithstanding the official terms of the inquiry, with these questions up-permost in the investigators' minds, it seemed privately a consensus formed early on amongst the surviving actors that the KLM captain, Jacob Van Zanten, had commenced his takeoff roll without clearance, and this was the primary cause of the catastrophe.

When the Pan Am representative asked Robert Bragg over the phone on the very day of the accident just what had happened, he had replied without hesitation, "a KLM jumbo took off without clearance and collided with us on the runway". Later, Bragg conferred with Warns and Grubbs in the hospital on Tenerife, and the three shared their thoughts on exactly what had taken place that afternoon.

I was very specific in telling the Captain (Grubbs) that I thought he had done everything he possibly could.

It was Bragg's opinion that had KLM hit the *Clipper* straight on, every-one would have perished—Grubb's quick decision to turn the plane to the left meant that some had been spared.

As Bragg did his rounds of the hospital floors, enquiring after the passen-gers, when they asked him what had happened, he kept giving them the same answer: I think KLM took off without clearance.

Perhaps such proclamations seem premature, even biased, but it appears that even before any investigation was under way, others in different camps agreed. The commander of the Spanish Airforce had already listened to the tower tapes with a view to establishing if Azcunaga may have been at fault. He went to see Bragg in the hospital to discuss his conclusions.

So he came in and he ... asked me what I thought had happened and I told him, I said "I think KLM took off without a clearance" and he said "do you think the tower had any blame for this accident" and I said "no, none whatsoever" and he said "I'm glad you said that because I've listened to the tower tapes ... and I don't think our tower was at fault."

Bragg confirmed with the commander that he had never heard Azcunaga issue a takeoff clearance to KLM.

Victor Grubbs seems to have suffered through a great deal of guilt and self-analysis following the disaster, turning over and over in his mind the question of whether he could—or should—have done something differently. Speaking from Walson Hospital at Fort Dix where he was transported for treatments to his burns, he told a reporter that in the end he had concluded he was not to blame.

Looking back at the rubble, I first thought to myself, look what I've done to these people. But in my heart, I know it wasn't my fault.

On 29 March, the actions of the Dutch pilot came sharply into focus after the press revealed that investigators had listened to the CVRs and tower tapes, and had concluded that Van Zanten had never been issued a takeoff clearance. Cor Westerneng, a KLM official, reluctantly conceded that there was no clearance, "but still the KLM plane took off." He averred, "We presume that there was a misunderstanding in the KLM cockpit regarding the position of the Pan American plane on the runway."

In the investigation to unfold, a chorus of Dutch voices would now join Westerneng's in raising a host of qualifiers and modifiers: it had been accepted that Van Zanten took off without clearance, but the question was, why? He had surely not done so deliberately, so his failure to correctly follow instructions must have had something to do with the actions of the Spanish and/or American parties to the disaster.

The Dutch found an ally in West Germany, whose head of airspace control, Wolfgang Kasserbohm, declared the unfitness of the airport and controllers at Los Rodeos: "flight safety systems there do not meet international standards."

Rumors began to circulate, later mentioned directly in the Dutch investigative report and a host of documentaries, that the tower controllers at Los Rodeos had been distracted by a football game on television when they were supposed to be attending to instructions to KLM and Pan Am. Azcunaga later strenuously denied these claims. They had, he said, been summoned out of thin air: there simply never was any television on in the controller's room.

Consider the fact that this notion that the controllers had been watching sport on TV instead of doing their jobs has been repeated in numerous accounts of this disaster, even highly publicized and commercial documentaries such as Mayday's *Crash of the Century*. Now consider the true origins of this story: it turns out that the first person to make the claim was actually the ringleader of the CIIM attack on Las Palmas. After the scale of the catastrophe was known, he was simply trying to deflect blame elsewhere for the unforeseen results of CIIM's actions. After that, the rumor simply caught on, and the Dutch leveraged it for their own benefit.

In Amsterdam, on 29 March, KLM President Sergio Orlandini vigorously expressed his view that he was in no doubt that the Dutch pilot would never have intentionally taken off without express permission from the tower. His statement was in part a counter-attack to words publicly issued by a Spanish aviation official to the effect that Van Zanten had ignored instructions "in plain English" to hold his position at the end of the runway.

Thus, with KLM's reputation on the line before the press and public, not to mention the massive financial penalties that would accrue should the crew of the *Rhine* be found responsible, the Dutch authorities set out to present their own evidence casting doubt upon any assertion that the actions of Van Zanten—KLM's star pilot—had been solely responsible for the disaster. The Final Report of the Netherlands Aviation Safety Board, in an effort to deflect attention from the role any recklessness or errors of judgment on the part of the Dutch pilot may have played in the collision, instead gave weight to Pan Am's failure to exit the runway via taxiway C-3, the effect of the simultaneous transmissions which rendered key parts of the communications from Pan Am and the tower inaudible, and the allegedly confusing instructions of the tower controllers, stated in non-standard and ambiguous terminology.

With regard to Pan Am missing their turn off, the Dutch report presents this as an "operational deviation", that is, an instance of the Pan Am crew having done the wrong thing, of failing to heed instructions. It did not take seriously the proposition that a plane of the *Clipper*'s size could not have navigated the angles of the turn.

The Dutch Safety Board even went so far as to conduct tests with their own pilots operating similar craft in an effort to demonstrate the *Clipper* could have successfully made the awkwardly angled turn onto C-3, that would have had them facing back in the direction of the obstructed parking apron. "Performance calculations and taxi tests with a B-747 turning off on an intersection comparable to the C3 at Tenerife, as part of the Netherlands investigation, indicate that in all probability no collision, and certainly no fatal collision would have occurred if the Pan Am aircraft had not taxied farther than the third intersection, which was emphatically instructed by the tower controller." The report concludes that even though Pan Am had attempted, unsuccessfully, to clarify their position on the runway, the fact that they had lingered there too long contrary to their directions was "a causal coincidence to the ultimate fatal collision."

The Dutch authorities attempted to impugn the claims of the Pan Am crew that, due to the fog and the absence of taxiway markings on their map of the airport, they had little chance of correctly identifying what exactly the controller meant by "the third" turn to the left of the runway, asserting that the CVR showed unequivocally that they had received the instruction to take the third exit before they had passed, and correctly identified, C1. Bragg had stated that he was convinced the controller intended for them to take the fourth exit because the instruction had arrived after they had passed the first exit. The truth of this matter has never been conclusively resolved. At any rate, Bragg himself considered the issue academic and ultimately irrelevant, because had Van Zanten not taken off without clearance, it would not have mattered that Pan Am missed their turn.

This, in fact, is the key point, and those on the other side had already come to the same—very reasonable—conclusion. The official American and Spanish reports regarded the fact that Pan Am had missed their turn as a contributing, but not causative factor in the disaster. Instead, these reports were focused more heavily on the motivations and behavior of Van Zanten himself. The key question was, why had he taken off without clearance? The answer, as far as the U.S. Airline Pilots Association who authored the American report were concerned, was the duty time restrictions and Van Zanten's desire to escape Los Rodeos before visibility worsened.

In short, he was in a hurry—and because he was in a hurry, he got careless, and nearly six hundred people died.

The ALPA report also considered the influence of the captain's relative lack of recent real-world flying experience at the time of the accident, his senior position with the airline, and the possibility that his subordinates in the cockpit had not felt comfortable with challenging his decisions. That finding from the report spurred the development of CRM (Crew Resource Management) and its adoption throughout the commercial aviation industry in the interests of safety.

The official conclusion when all views were taken into account, all evidence analyzed and weighed, and all investigations completed, was that Van Zanten had caused the accident by taking off without clearance.

The Spanish Report concluded that:

"The fundamental cause of this accident was the fact that the KLM Captain:

1. Took off without clearance.

2. Did not obey the "stand by for takeoff" instruction from the tower.

3. Did not interrupt takeoff on learning that Pan Am was still on the runway.

4. In reply to the Flight Engineer's query as to whether Pan Am, had already left the runway, replied emphatically in the affirmative..

These words do sound rather damning, but to some degree they take the findings out of the report's full context.

Let us be perfectly clear that nobody—at any time, even the Spanish—were saying that Van Zanten took off without clearance on purpose. Instead, it is accepted (although it cannot be conclusively proven, because we cannot ask Van Zanten himself) that he thought he had clearance when he did not.

That misapprehension was mostly a result of the communication failures with Pan Am and the tower, caused by the heterodyne and the use of nonstandard terminology by both KLM and the tower. Secondarily, it seems that due to Van Zanten's haste and irritability—which can be clearly detected in his voice on the recording—he was operating in an altered and impaired state of situational awareness. And because he was in that suboptimal state of awareness, he was simply more likely to convince himself of things that were not true, and interpret ambiguous information in a way that was favorable to the outcome he was seeking.

Let us consider for a moment the proposition that Van Zanten had purposefully taken off without clearance. One might gain this impression from the many dramatic American produced documentaries about this crash, with their caricature of the Dutch captain as an overbearing, know-it-all cockpit tyrant.

To say that Van Zanten knowingly took off without clearance, while aware there was even a sliver of a chance that Pan Am were still on the runway, is to say that he is a murderer.

There have been, throughout history, examples of suicidal and murderous pilots who wantonly endangered the lives of their passengers. In 1994, a pilot flying a Royal Air Maroc turboprop loaded with 44 passengers disconnected the autopilot and deliberately crashed his plane into a mountainside soon after takeoff. All aboard died. Most recently the 2015 crash of Germanwings Flight 9525 brought wide media attention to this issue. Co-pilot Andreas Lubitz was known to suffer from depression and had been declared "unfit for work" before he locked his captain in the bathroom and deliberately sabotaged his plane, killing all 144 people on board.

The Dutch captain was most certainly not one of these pilots. Nothing we know about the man, his character, values and priorities squares with that possibility. He was a senior, highly respected pilot at KLM. He erred due to his worries about financial and reputational threats faced by his airline. Why on earth would he deliberately takeoff without clearance?

And yet, despite the decided reality that this was an exemplary and competent man who made one very grave mistake, thinly-veiled condemnation rained down on the Dutch captain from almost all sides at the time of the accident, and has continued to do so in the years since.

A relative of an American victim, who has chosen to keep their identity undisclosed, was vociferous and unequivocal in their opinion. "He [Van Zanten] is a killer".

Ironically, in the years since the accident, Captain Van Zanten has had more ire heaped on him within aviation and piloting communities than men who willfully endangered the lives of their passengers. One aviation enthusiast asked on a public forum, "Why did Captain Van Zanten kill 583 with his KLM 747?"—almost as if the man was indeed a butcher, and the plane his weapon! The commenter continued, "[he] knew himself that the official "cleared for takeoff" transmission hadn't been issued by the tower! ... but the captain decided it was time to go."

An article posted online about the Tenerife disaster is entitled: *A horror tale of how one man's arrogance killed 583 people.* "He had a problem with authority", opines the writer. "He was a man who did not like to be second-guessed."

To understand the level of denunciation against Van Zanten, it is necessary to have an appreciation for the fundamentals of airmanship all good pilots hold so dear. From their perspective, it is perhaps worse to be a competent pilot who made such an egregious error as Van Zanten did, than to be a callow murderer or a reckless amateur.

Why? Every pilot knows that taking off without clearance is one of the most unforgivable errors you can make. And ask pretty much any commercial pilot whether, based on the evidence, Van Zanten should have known the ATC clearance he was given was not a takeoff clearance, and they will say unequivocally that the answer is yes. He should have known this.

The fact that he dismissed his flight engineer Willem Schreuder when he tried to bring the fact that Pan Am was still on the runway to his attention—and when a statement to this effect from the tower was also audible in the KLM cockpit—compounds the outrageousness of the captain's mistake to a point that it almost strains credulity. The question then arises, how could anyone make such mistakes "by accident"? Their answer is that Van Zanten's "errors" simply spoke to an impatience and recklessness in his character that—considered in light of the moral responsibilities of his role— make him ethically responsible for 583 deaths, even if he did not willfully harm a single person.

Robert Firth, former commercial pilot and author of *Aftermath*, posed this question in his discussion of the disaster: "Would I have made the same mistake? In all honesty, given the same scenario I think I would not ... knowing, as Van Zanten most definitely did, that Pan Am was following me as I back-taxied for takeoff, I would not have moved until I was absolutely certain the runway was clear".

* * *

There is another angle on this disaster that holds the Dutch captain responsible not necessarily in a moral way, but simply because his decision to takeoff was the final link in the chain. Essentially, there were numerous unfortunate co-incidences that set up the conditions for the catastrophe, but had Van Zanten not taken-off prematurely, those conditions would have been simply irrelevant—and none of them would have predicted any loss of life.

This disaster has frequently been explained with reference to the so-called Swiss Cheese Model theory of accident causation. Initially embraced as a risk model within the field of nuclear energy, the theory has subsequently been adopted by aviation, space, healthcare and other complex organizations where human safety considerations are paramount. Where earlier models tended to assume accidents resulted from a chain of events flowing on one from the other, this model proposes that there exist many causes for potential errors in reliable organizations that at times occur independently of one another. The accident only occurs if all of the "holes" of the Swiss cheese are aligned.

Here, the "cheese" was the possibility of our crews and passengers safely getting out of Los Rodeos airport, into the skies, and onto Las Palmas. And up until the moment when Jacob Van Zanten started his calamitous roll down the runway, our protagonists had already been plagued by several unfortunate alignments of the holes in their cheese.

Here are our "holes":

- Terrorist attack on Las Palmas and the fact that aircraft have been diverted to Tenerife in the first place. Pan Am were refused permission for a holding pattern which forced them to land at Tenerife.

- The size and condition of the airport, not designed to accommodate many large aircraft, and requiring backtaxi maneuvers to get planes back into the air.

- Communication difficulties between the controllers and the cockpit crews.

- Use of non-standard phraseology and confusion about taxi instructions.

- The absence of ground radar at Los Rodeos, meaning that the controllers were largely ignorant of the crews' actual position on the runway and taxiways.

- KLM's duty time limits, and their decision to refuel, a decision which created a delay during which visibility worsened, and detained the departure of the Pan American.

- Captain Grubbs voiced an early preference to hold at the entry point to the runway until KLM had taken off, instead of taxing and turning into a charlie taxiway, but the request was not followed up by Bragg and was not communicated to the controllers.

- The fog bound condition of the runway, the inability of the crews to see each other's vessels or the surrounding airport terrain, and following on from that, the fact that the Pan American ship missed the correct turn off the runway.

The coincidence of all these events, by itself, represents an almost inconceivable chain of bad luck. Our men already seemed to be chained subordinates to the dictates of Murphy's Law.

But then, one final—and colossally unfortunate—twist of fate sealed the deal. The heterodyne cancelled out both Pan Am's warning to Van Zanten that they were still on the runway—as well as the controller's instruction to "stand by" for takeoff. The nail in the coffin was in sad fact the perverse result of the Pan American crew's last-ditch effort to clear up the communication mishap, and save everyone's lives.

That this occurred is mind-blowingly unlucky. It almost beggars belief. If someone wrote a fictional account with the same facts, one probably wouldn't even believe it. But this was not fiction; it was reality.

Van Zanten had one final opportunity to avert disaster though, and he did not take it. His crew mates warned him of potential trouble ahead—but he did not listen.

It isn't clear why Schreuder heard the controller saying to the Pan Am crew over radio, "report when runway clear"—the message that tipped him off that there was danger ahead—when Van Zanten and Meurs apparently did not. This is another reason why the captain has been so roundly condemned.

As one aviation enthusiast said, *I just cannot understand why he continued to roll after hearing that Pan Am were still on the runway.*

The prevailing wisdom is that Van Zanten did not hear it, being distracted by the technicalities of takeoff. Ultimately, however, what he heard or did not hear is a matter of speculation. But, taken together, the fact that there had been a garbled radio transmission, and that he had been warned by his own Flight Officer, should have been sufficient information for him to abort takeoff. He would have had time to do so, as the radio message asking Pan Am to report when clear of the runway was received just seconds after Van Zanten pushed forward on the throttles. But he did not abort.

And it seems that he did not, because his attention was firmly fixed on leaving Tenerife.

Perhaps Van Zanten has been such a figure of controversy because ultimately, while his actions were deadly, they are still are somewhat mysterious. We do not know what he was thinking. We cannot ask him. And in the darkness, we can only speculate.

Some of those speculations get rather grim. We know he was in a hurry. Is it possible that because he was in a hurry, he simply filtered out the undesirable information that was telling him he shouldn't take off yet?

This train of thought is the stuff of pilots' nightmares, and I believe that is the real reason why the Dutch captain is such a provocative figure. For while we judge him, can we really say that we would have made the right choice under the circumstances with which he was faced?

He is facing major headaches if he does not get off the ground. He could be facing prosecution if his crew exceed their duty time limit. And if he isn't going to risk that, he must find accommodation for all his passengers overnight on Tenerife, which, from where he is standing, seems almost a logistical impossibility.

Put yourself in his shoes. With all this on your mind, can you say with any certainty that you wouldn't begin interpreting the confusing information around you in a way that is favorable to the outcome you want? Would you really not make the same mistake?

A very good discussion of human factors in the causation of this accident has been provided by McCreary, Pollard, Stevenson and Wilson of the Aviation Institute at the University of Nebraska in their article *Tenerife Revisited*. They note that the results of stress, anxiety and irritability in team environments tends to be that a range of perceived alternatives is likely to narrow—but not necessarily to the best option. Decision making under such conditions tends to become centralized, falling back on authoritarian lines of control, with an accompanying loss of creativity, flexibility and cooperation.

Team actors will also likely to be fall into regressive behaviors, that is, the reliance on familiar solutions that have worked in the past. Most importantly, under conditions of stress and information deficit, where the data needed to make a decision is unclear or incomplete, team actors will suffer a reduced tolerance for ambiguity and complexity. They'll tend to cut off their information searching, and lock in a premature decision.

Van Zanten, the authors ominously assert, "responded to the stresses of time and weather by literally shutting all other players, including the ATC officers, out of his decision-making loop."

Let us consider this idea for a moment, and turn it over in our minds. As an explanation for the captain's actions, it is compelling; but it also raises the confronting specter of moral ambivalence. The question of whether or not he was a "killer" or not misses the point. The logical conclusion is that Van Zanten behaved recklessly, but that recklessness was natural in the situation, and anybody might have behaved in exactly the same way—in fact, under conditions of stress in complex environments, where an important decision must be made, this is often exactly how people behave.

The analysis takes morality and ethical responsibility out of the equation, and the implications are disturbing, leaving us with a sense of the precariousness of life, the tangential and chaotic nature of our existence in the world.

The captain's actions, which destroyed the lives of hundreds of human beings, were the wrong ones—but they were motivated by the very human desire to maintain control and get the right outcome in a situation fraught with complexity.

The truth is that none of us—even the most exemplary and accomplished—have nearly as much control as we think we do. The vagaries of our psychology can get the better of us, at any moment: and at worst, in the most critical of moment of our life.

Perhaps that is what pilots find so very chilling about this accident. It carries with it a message that no pilot wants to hear: that no matter their level of skills, training and knowledge, or their good intentions, their human instincts could lead them far astray in the crucial hour ... with deadly consequences.

Calling Van Zanten a murderer lets us off the hook. It helps us maintain the illusion of control, and protects us from a much more harrowing possibility—that none of us know what we might do when the stakes are so high, and the outcome is dependent on us making the right call.

Postscript

Today we are four decades away from the events of that ghastly afternoon on 27 March 1977, when hundreds of European and American tourists descended on paradise for the holiday of a lifetime, and instead were burnt to cinders in the most unexpected and terrifying way.

The most commonly discussed legacy of this accident is its subsequent influence on the international commercial aviation industry. I believe some of the hype about the comprehensiveness of that influence is misplaced. There are some misconceptions around about how Tenerife was some kind of "blessing in disguise". I will do my best to clear these up.

The fact that the cockpit discipline of CRM was only widely implemented as a result of this crash is well-known, and no doubt has made a vitally important contribution to safety.

Certainly a key causal factor in Van Zanten's decision to takeoff prematurely was the fact that his subordinates in the cockpit did not feel one-hundred percent confident to forcefully object to his decisions, when they knew all was not necessarily well on the ground. Meurs knew that Van Zanten did not have a clearance, but chose not to say anything about it; and Schreuder knew that Pan Am was still on the runway, but could only find it within himself to speak up once, thereafter letting the matter rest, to the peril of everyone. The captain, by the same token, did not feel compelled to listen to the objections that his teammates *did* voice. The development and deployment of CRM throughout the industry was meant to correct this. Today, all commercial airlines mandate a more democratic cockpit culture and pilots are encouraged to challenge a captain's decisions when to do so is in the interests of safety. Captains are also required to listen and take on any such feedback in their decision-making process.

Somewhat less known is that prior to Tenerife, it was fairly common for pilots and controllers to communicate using non-standardized phraseology, and this too was an important contributor to the disaster. For example, Meurs message to the controller that the KLM was "uh, at takeoff", was interpreted by Azcunaga to mean that he was holding in takeoff position. As a result, today, these communications have been standardized to prescribe that the words "takeoff" are only to be used by pilots and controllers when a specific take-off clearance is being requested or issued. Another major contributor to this accident was that KLM combined their request for the ATC and takeoff clearance, which generated confusion all round. Regulations now require that a pilot (if circumstances permit) must not request a taxi clearance until after he or she has requested, received and read back a departure instruction or en-route clearance.

What hardly anybody is aware of is that the phenomenon of heterodyne—the effect of simultaneous transmissions blocking important messages between tower and cockpit crews—is still a grave threat to safety in commercial aviation. The fact that Van Zanten neither heard Pan Am's warning that they were on the runway, nor the controllers instruction to stand by, was really the final stroke of terrible luck that sealed the deal in the causation of this catastrophe. And as of today, little has actually been done to prevent a repeat!

People often ask, "Could Tenerife happen again?" This is the wrong question. Tenerife has *already happened again.* It was just that these incidents, purely by chance, happened to be smaller in scale, and not deadly—therefore, less noteworthy. In fact, while other types of accidents have decreased in recent memory, the number of runway incursion incidents—where planes collide, touch or have a near-miss on the ground—have increased, largely due to the more congested conditions in most airports. In the late 1990s, the FAA reported that there had been a doubling of the number of runway incursions just in the few years from 1992 to 1996. A number of these incidents were caused by radio-frequency saturation causing squeals and call-sign clipping, leading to misinterpretation of reports and instructions.

Following on from this report, concern over the issue within the aviation industry was on the rise, and the FAA encouraged airlines to adopt a new technology called CONTRAN, a VHF anti-blocking device that monitors VHF channels and prevents a pilot or controller from speaking onto an already busy frequency. Two commercial airliners did adopt the technology—Britannia, a major UK charter operator, and Virgin Atlantic. But for reasons unknown, other major airlines never followed suit.

CONTRAN and related technologies are a basic and rather inexpensive solution to an old and worrying problem. *Salon* aviation writer More P. Smith has remarked that "the fix is so low-tech, in fact, the airlines and regulators should be ashamed and embarrassed even to debate the matter."

Certainly, with the events of Tenerife foremost in mind, knowing that this most elementary safety feature has never been implemented in the cockpits of the majority of commercial aircraft gives me no comfort any time I step onto an airplane.

The received wisdom in commercial aviation is that people have to die in order for investigators and regulators to understand exactly what can go wrong, and what changes need to be made, in order to prevent future tragedies. But the formal narrative of this disaster, emphasizing its historic legacy of crucial lessons learned in the interests of passenger safety, obscures the brutal truth that many preventable causes of this accident remain at play in commercial aviation incidents to this very day.

Poor situational awareness in low visibility, communications mix ups and inadequate airport markings of runway and taxiway entries and exits were factors in several notable airplane crashes that occurred well after Tenerife, including the Lexington Comair Flight 5191 crash in 2006, the Singapore Airlines Flight 006 crash in Taipei in 2000, and the Linate Airport disaster in Milan in 2001—another horrific example of a runway incursion.

Leaving aside the technical and mechanical causes of air crashes, human factors are a persistent and immovable issue, despite the adoption of CRM principles. Gerald M. Bruggink, a former Deputy Director of the NTSB, believes that the primary cause of the Tenerife disaster was that the central actors proceeded on the basis of assumptions which they did not bother to test.

Pilots still make these very mortal mistakes today. "No amount of technological progress in the new century can alter the role of the human factor in the aviation system."

* * *

The more compelling legacy of this disaster, to me, is something less tangible than the effects on the airline industry.

Over the years a mythology has grown up around Tenerife, made up of all the televisual accounts of the accident. The dominant story of this event is one of American heroism. Pan Am were the good guys; KLM were the villains. The truth is much more layered. While it is common knowledge that KLM were reluctant to accept full responsibility for the disaster, most people don't know that the Dutch authorities showed great dignity and generosity in handling the compensation of the victims' families, paying the sum of $58,000 for each with no hesitation once the official findings were in, in line with their responsibilities under a pact made in Warsaw in 1929. KLM also advised the families of the victims to appoint their own lawyers, at the company's cost. Some families were paid large additional compensation sums in recognition of their unique circumstances: one received the amount of $400,000, because the victim was the families' sole breadwinner. One man wanted to travel to Australia to speak with his family about the disaster, and was given a free air ticket.

On the other hand, there were some embarrassing revelations for Pan Am when Robert Bragg spoke for the first time about his memorable time during those few days on Tenerife. This thread of the story, which is not common knowledge, is almost farcical. Bragg alleged that when he was calling Pan Am's offices in the United States after the accident to update them on the emerging information and the headcount of survivors, not only did they not take most of his calls, they didn't bother to call him back. Their excuse was that "in a situation like this, certain things get forgotten."

It wasn't good enough, Bragg remarked.

But there was more, and worse, to come. Pan Am were meant to send a representative to meet Bragg and the small group of survivors he travelled back to London with at Las Palmas. The representative was to organize their connection and escort them back to the UK. The rep arrived at Las Palmas and greeted the group, but promptly wandered off into the terminal, never to return. As a result, the group missed their connection and had to wait for the next one out. Peter Jennings, who was travelling with this group, ended up arranging the tickets.

Pan Am put Bragg in a hotel for the night once he arrived in London. At this point he still had only the clothes he'd been wearing on the plane to put on his back. Pan Am had promised to get him whatever he needed.

They got me a sweater, a pair of beach sandals, a pair of men's underwear which I could not possibly get on they were so small, one toothbrush with no toothpaste and one razor without a razorblade ... and I got back to the States, the Vice President of Operations Evan Mulligan had to loan me his blue jacket, a guy about six inches taller than I was loaned me his pants and another guy loaned me his shirt ... I looked like the proverbial hobo.

So much for American heroism. Keep in mind this was not only an employee of Pan Am, but one of their top pilots—not to mention a man who had just been through an absolutely horrendous experience—who was subjected to such treatment.

As it happened, Pan American World Airways collapsed just fifteen years later. That had nothing directly to do with Tenerife, but was widely thought to be the fallout of an over-aggressive strategy of growth and a lapse into the same attitudes of arrogance and hubris that KLM have been accused of in so many documentaries about the Tenerife tragedy. The world's oldest airline KLM, on the other hand, is still running today and despite whatever reputational damage Tenerife caused it, it maintains its solid reputation for safety, efficiency and great customer service.

I say all this by means of showing that the true story of Tenerife is so much more nuanced and ambiguous than the formal accounts will have you believe, and it is within this complexity that the truth and beauty of this tragedy lies, if we can even speak of such a thing.

The inside story of this disaster is one of mistakes and mishandling on all sides. Its truth is a potent witness to the folly and imperfection of human nature, and puts paid to our overblown confidence in the proudest of commercial institutions.

Certainly, such tragedies can be a great social leveler, revealing in the end the shared quality of our humanity—both our noblest, and much less dignified, traits.

* * *

In the years since it happened, the power of the Tenerife disaster to haunt, disturb and fascinate has never diminished. For aviation insiders and the general public alike, it exerts a lingering morbid captivation, perhaps not only because of the scale of the tragedy, but because the way in which it unfolded almost seems to defy comprehension.

There's bad luck and misfortune in life ... but then, there's what happened that afternoon. As author and pilot Patrick Smith remarked, "one of the only things that will hush a room full of pilots is a video or a presentation about what happened at Tenerife ... all the bizarre coincidences and twisted ironies that were part of that crash ... all the horror, but at the same time, this weird mystique ..."

Unsurprisingly, enthusiasts of conspiracy and the paranormal are amongst those who have attempted to develop their own explanations for this crash, the freakish details of which on so many levels seem to fly in the face of logical interpretation. They wonder, as we all do, just how it was that such an extremely unfortunate chain of incidents could come together in one place and time, with such a devastating outcome.

Was it something about the date? Something about Tenerife itself? There are those who think that there was some kind of supernatural or mystical influence at work. Attempts to theorize the 9-11 disaster by numerology are renowned, and likewise there are the outliers who have explored the esoteric dimensions of 27 March 1977.

A practitioner of Chinese numerology writes, "1977 was a year of the snake. The snake carries the meaning of malevolence, cattiness and mystery, as well as acumen and divination ... this animal is considered evil. In a year of the snake there are always many disasters." Indeed, there is a long list of other aviation accidents that occurred in 1977, including the TAP Portugal Flight 425 crash at Madeira Airport, in which 131 people died, the Malaysia Airlines Flight 653 hijacking and subsequent crash in Tanjung Kupang, Malaysia, in which all 100 passengers and crew on board lost their lives, and the well-known and tragic incident in which A DC-3 charter plane carrying the University of Evansville basketball team to Nashville, Tennessee, crashed in rain and dense fog some 90 seconds after takeoff from Evansville Dress Regional Airport, and most of the team including coach Bob Watson perished.

The numerological calculation of the date on which the Tenerife crash occurred is the number 9, which is yielded by adding and then condensing the numbers. Number 9 is a number signifying completion, finality, and the end of a cycle. Being that it is concerned with ending, it also contains resonances of death and destruction. We will note, as well, the significance and repetition of the number 9 in the twin towers disaster.

Numerology of course, for many, is not an explanatory science but merely an occult exercise of idle speculation. But numerologists are not alone in thinking there was something hinky and mystical about this disaster.

Tales and rumors of haunting at Los Rodeos airport are also rife.

A website entitled "Paranormal activity at Los Rodeos" cites testimony of several airport workers who have reported seeing screaming ghosts trying to jump from actual, working planes on the runway. They have also described seeing passenger's ghosts running from the tarmac around the accident site onto the grass, as if they were still trying to escape the burning Pan Am jet years and years later.

A former pilot has this tale to tell: "one guy I regularly flew with (until quite recently) spent considerable time flying in and out of Tenerife ... [he] was adamant that the spirits of the long departed would discriminately appear in large numbers on the Tenerife tarmac. He claims that he's delayed two takeoffs because of what he thought were figures on the runway waving their hands as if to warn departing aircraft of impending danger."

* * *

In Mesa Mota Park on the outskirts of the city of San Cristobal La Laguna on Tenerife, where the ecumenical memorial service for the dead was held all those years ago on 30 March 1977, the majestic International Tenerife Memorial soars high into the azure skies, commanding expansive views of Los Rodeos airport below, and in the hazy distance, volcanic Mount Teide, the tallest mountain is Spanish territory.

Like the disaster it commemorates, the symbolism of this stunning memorial is ambiguous and open to interpretation. Designed by Dutch artist Rudi Van de Wint, it is in the form of a towering spiral staircase connecting the earth to the skies. As such it is suggestive of the ascent to heaven, an appropriate and consoling motif for all those who came to such an otherwise undignified end.

Others have noted another figurative connotation. It is also reminiscent of the spiral staircases that connected the upper first-class cabins to the main decks in the early models of Boeing 747 jumbos, of which *Clipper* and *Rhine* were examples.

The inauguration of this monument was heavily attended by relatives of those who lost their lives, and it has continued to give comfort to the survivors and the families of the victims in the decades since. One of these is Jan

Groenewould, a Dutch national who at just 22 years old lost his entire family in the crash. A founding member of Foundation Relatives Victims Tenerife, his efforts were instrumental in bringing about the agreement between the Dutch Foreign Office and authorities in Tenerife which set the plans for the monument into action.

I became an adult in ten seconds, Groenewould recalls of the tragedy, which had an "enormous impact" on him. With the support of his 86-year-old grandmother, he eventually learned to live with the pain. He says that today he can't abide to waste time, and is determined to live every day to the fullest. *You have to go on with your life.*

Groenwould is very happy with the memorial that finally resulted from his desire to see a formal commemorative site established.

However the monument's meaning is interpreted by the individual, it is obviously a representation of the notion of infinity, of the persistence of spirit. Rudi Van de Wint elucidated the meaning of his creation with these stirring words:

"People either like or dislike a monument, but a monument is about so much more. The ritual significance of the location is of prime importance. Monuments are often places of yearning; they are projections of impotence, of the brokenness of the human spirit and of the universal drama. A monument which encapsulates a yearning for reconciliation or acceptance can never be too sober, because the real drama cannot be expressed in art. Art can only provide a subtle hint ..."

Tenerife is truly exemplary of the ineffable, one of those historical moments that brings us into confrontation with all about existence that can never be fully touched or comprehended. Certainly, for those who lived through that terrible afternoon of 27 March 1977, no artistic or literary attempt to capture its meaning will ever quite hit the mark. For her part, all this author could do was try.

Books by OJ Modjeska

Did you enjoy *Gone: Catastrophe in Paradise*? Remember to subscribe to OJ's mailing list at the link below to receive notifications of new releases. And if amazing true stories are your cup of tea, please do check out OJ's new two-part true crime series, *Murder by Increments*. Book One, *A City Owned*, and Book Two, *Killing Cousins*, are both out now.

http://ojmodjeska.blogspot.com.au

www.estoire.co

One after another, they appear by the sides of suburban roads and free-ways – the naked, strangled bodies of women who have been raped, tor-tured and left for dead. Police begin to suspect that their target is a rogue operator who has emerged from their own ranks. And then, all hell breaks loose in Los Angeles... An arrest in the strangling murders of two co-eds across state lines finally leads to a break in the case, but the mild-mannered suspect remembers nothing about the crime of which he is accused. His attorney and a team of psychiatrists are convinced this is no lust murderer, but a mentally ill man tormented by an evil alter personality, the terrifyingly malevolent sexual sadist "Steve". But what if Steve is the final triumphant act in a psychopath's lifelong career in deception? None are prepared for the dark journey through the mazes of the human mind it will take to unlock the door to justice.

From the author of the aviation disaster ebook bestseller "Gone: Catas-trophe in Paradise", "Murder by Increments" is the true story of the worst case of serial sex homicide in American history.

Made in the USA
San Bernardino, CA
03 November 2019

59364741R00054